HIRED!

Empowering Parents with 6 Simple Steps to Support Your Child in Getting a Job!

HEATHER RYBARUK

Hired!
Empowering Parents with 6 Simple Steps to Support Your Child in Getting a Job
© 2024 Heather Rybaruk

ISBN: 9781068661907 Paperback

Published by: Inspired By Publishing

Cover design by: Tanya Grant – The TNG Designs Group Limited

Acknowledgements

Writing a book is a journey, and I am forever grateful to the incredible people who have supported me along the way. Without their steadfast encouragement, guidance, and belief in me, this book would not have been possible.

First and foremost, I want to express my deepest gratitude to my amazing husband, Steve. Your unconditional love, patience, and understanding have been my rock throughout this process. Without your support, I wouldn't have been able to achieve this milestone.

To my superstar son Seb, thank you for being by my side, writing alongside me, and inspiring me with your own literary aspirations. I have no doubt that your best-seller is just around the corner.

I am truly blessed to have a circle of friends who have kept me going and believed in my ability to achieve this. Your unwavering faith and constant motivation have been invaluable.

To my Dad, thank you for your "pedantic" critiques – they have undoubtedly made this book better. And to my Mum, your unreserved support in whatever I do means the world to me.

I am incredibly fortunate to have a team that not only puts up with my ability to break things but also celebrates my successes. LT and Emiki, your steadfast support has been invaluable.

Dave, my recruitment agent and friend for 20 years, your advice and support over the years have been instrumental in shaping my understanding of the recruitment world and what is possible.

I am truly grateful to my networking group, Quantock Referral, for their unflinching support throughout this project. Special mentions go to Carolyn, Dave, Gavin, and David for their honest feedback in the final stages.

To Karen Matthews, where this all started – thank you for reaching out on LinkedIn and sending me your CV to review. Your trust in me has been the catalyst for the hundreds of people who have put their faith in me to help them make a difference. The success stories I have now are just the beginning, and I am truly honoured to be a part of people's journeys.

Finally, I would like to express my sincere gratitude to Chloë and her team at Inspired By Publishing. Your hard work and dedication have made this book a reality, and the impact you have on people's lives is truly remarkable.

Thank you, one and all, for being a part of this incredible journey. Your support and belief in me have been the driving force behind this book, and I am forever grateful.

Contents

Introduction

My name is Heather Rybaruk, and I am fueled by both passion and parenthood. As an HR and career strategist, as well as a devoted mother, I am on a mission to empower the next generation in their journey towards employment. I understand the challenges parents face in navigating their children's career paths, which is why I am here to offer guidance and support.

Think of me not just as a typical parenting guide, but as a career strategist, coach and mentor, who will provide you with this comprehensive Six-Step Strategy that will help you effectively guide your child towards securing meaningful employment.

Throughout this book, I will share my two decades of experience in HR and recruitment to provide you with insights into what employers are looking for in candidates, and what common mistakes to avoid during the application and interview process.

By understanding the perspective of HR and recruitment professionals, you can better support your child in positioning themselves for success in their roles.

My journey in both large corporations and small businesses has led me to wear many hats, but my role as a passionate mentor has been the most fulfilling. I own my HR Consultancy and am driven by a profound passion for unlocking the untapped potential within every individual. This work allows me to help small to medium businesses scale and grow by understanding the talent they have, aligning them to the company's mission and values, and creating succession planning for retention and growth.

Through this book, I share insights and strategies that extend beyond traditional parenting, aiming to guide you in unleashing your child's full potential. As we go through the steps of this strategy, we will explore the critical role you play as a parent in shaping your child's career choices, and introduce supporting tasks and activities that can be used for the rest of their careers.

As we navigate through the chapters, you will discover how your engagement can be a transformative force in shaping your child's career aspirations. Throughout this Six-Step Strategy, I am committed to provide you with the tools and knowledge necessary to navigate the complexities of career guidance.

Together, let us unlock the talents within your child and set them on a trajectory for success. The journey starts here, with your active participation and a shared vision for your child's prosperous future.

The Importance of Parental Involvement

Let us confront the reality that many children now don't know what to do or how to transition from student to employee. For example, say you hear your child say they want to be a YouTube star. It looks easy and simple enough to do, so why can't they do that?

My son is 8 and wants to be a professional football player. Do I tell him the reality that less than 1% make it to play football as a career? Many careers still involve football even if he doesn't make it. I am not going to crush his dream; just encourage him that commitment and practice will bring him closer to his dream to develop and grow as a player.

You also encounter University graduates who veer away from their intended career paths, because they don't know how to get a job related to their studies. While there are many resources in the University, most students don't utilise or maximise their tutors' or career support to enable them to reach their full potential.

Statistics tell us 67% of children enter their initial jobs based on their parents' choices, while 49% of university graduates turn away from their studied fields due to uncertainties. These numbers highlight the undeniable influence parents have on their children's career trajectories and, in turn, the responsibility we bear in guiding them effectively. The decisions made during the formative years can significantly impact a child's professional choices, and as a parent, you have the power to guide them towards a successful and fulfilling career.

In order to support your child effectively in their job search journey, it is crucial to uphold certain commitments that will empower them to make informed decisions, discover their strengths and interests, and navigate the job market with confidence. Here are the commitments your child needs from you in order to get hired:

Active Listening

Take the time to actively listen to your child's thoughts, interests, and aspirations. Create a supportive environment where they feel comfortable sharing their ideas and concerns. Don't judge, just listen.

Encourage

Create a safe environment where they can be open to research career options for themselves. Help your child identify their strengths, interests, and values, allowing them to make informed decisions about their career path and help their self development.

Provide Guidance, Not Pressure

Offer guidance without imposing your own aspirations on your child. Allow them to explore various options and make decisions based on their own interests and passions rather than external pressures.

Explore Diverse Experiences

Encourage your child to engage in diverse experiences, internships, or volunteer opportunities. Exposure to different fields can help them discover new interests and gain valuable insights into potential career paths. Experience is not only valuable on the CV, it gives them an idea of what they do and don't like, and what possible shifts, roles, duties, and responsibilities, for which they have the potential.

Facilitate Networking Opportunities

Understand your network opportunity and seek advice or introduce your child to professionals in fields of interest. Networking can provide valuable insights, mentorship, and a realistic view of various careers.

Support Goal Setting

Assist your child in setting realistic and achievable job hunting and career goals. Break down large goals into smaller, manageable steps, empowering them to make progress toward their aspirations.

Promote Resilience

Teach your child the importance of resilience and adaptability. The career journey may involve setbacks, and it's crucial for them to learn how to overcome challenges and stay focused on their goals.

Respect Individual Choices

Recognise that your child's career choices may not align with your own expectations. Respect their individuality and support them in pursuing a path that brings them fulfilment and happiness.

Become a Source of Emotional Support

Job searching and career decisions can be challenging. Be there for them, offering encouragement and understanding during this significant phase of your child's life. Then when they get hired, celebrate!!!!!! Really praise them. It's not the same world we found our job in.

By upholding these commitments, you can help your child develop the skills, mindset, and confidence necessary to succeed in their career. It's important to remember that the job market and career development journey have changed significantly since our time, and it's crucial to support our children in navigating this new landscape. By creating a supportive and empowering environment, you can help your child discover their passions, develop their skills, and pursue a career that brings them fulfilment and happiness.

I am excited to share the Six-Step Strategy. If you or your child gets stressed or frustrated, go back to the commitments above. I have seen many coaches and leaders that talk about "if you stick to the plan or strategy it works." We all try to take short cuts or try to do it our own way. There's really no problem with that. And if you think you can get a shortcut into a job your child really wants, then please go ahead and take it.

My goal is to unlock talent and help your child get a job with your support. However, if it's not working out, do revisit the strategy and follow the process.

Why? Because it works.

People have tried to do things their own way, which I can support. But in my experience, it delays the process (time) and may affect their application (no interview or job offer). Don't give up and stay the course!

"Champions keep playing until they get it right."
– Billie Jean King

As a career coach and mentor with extensive experience in HR, recruitment, and learning and development, my goal is to support you in guiding your child towards a successful career. I am passionate about unlocking talent and helping the next generation get hired and enjoy their jobs! Helping your child secure a fulfilling role and achieve their career goals can be a rewarding and joyful experience. I hope that you get the same sense of jubilation that I do when my clients land a role, get a promotion, or pay rise. Let's work together to help your child succeed and enjoy collective success!

A Big Promise for Parents Wanting to Help Your Child Secure a Job in Just Six Steps!

Are you a parent worried about your child's job opportunities, frustrated by their lack of work experience, and nervous about their uncertain career path? I bring you a Six-Step Strategy designed for parents like you, ready to make a significant impact on their child's journey to professional success.

My promise is to guide you through a transformative experience that will empower you to confidently support your child in setting clear career goals, navigating the job market, and mastering the art of interviews. By the end of this program, you will experience a remarkable shift—from feeling overwhelmed and uncertain to being more confident, informed, and prepared.

I promise that, by the end of this Six-Step Strategy, you will be able to help your child:

1. **Understand how much do they need to earn, defining career goals**

   Step 1 will help clarify what your child wants and needs to earn, now and in future careers.

2. **Explore career options comprehensively**

   Step 2 enables them to dive deep into potential roles and industries, ensuring they gain a thorough understanding of opportunities that align with their aspirations using keywords to optimise their searches.

3. **Craft a standout CV**

   Step 3 is dedicated to creating a compelling and targeted CV that showcases your child's unique skills and experiences and captures hirers' attention.

4. **Expand professional networks**

   In Step 4, we guide your child in building a powerful professional network, understanding the opportunities they have and leveraging it to uncover jobs and gaining insights from seasoned professionals.

5. **Refine application skills**

   Step 5 focuses on honing your child's application skills, ensuring each one is tailored to specific roles, significantly boosting their chances of landing job interviews.

6. **Build confidence in interviews**

   Step 6 promises competitive-edge interview training, empowering your child to exude confidence, showcase their strengths, address weaknesses, and emerge as the standout candidate.

I understand the challenges you face as a concerned parent. My big promise is that, in just six steps, you'll witness a positive shift in your child's career trajectory. They will gain the confidence, skills, and purpose to navigate the professional world successfully. Get ready to offer support and guidance to help your child get their first job and learn tools and tips to use for the rest of their career! Being a parent, their success is your success!

"Dream big. Start small. But most of all, start."

\- Simon Sinek

Chapter 1
Step 1: Understand Your Child's Career Aspirations and Financial Needs

"Children are not things to be moulded but are people to be unfolded." – Jess Lair

Welcome to the beginning of our journey to help your child achieve their dream job. In this first chapter, we'll lay the groundwork for success with step one of the Six-Step Strategy.

Our focus here is on two vital aspects: understanding your child's career aspirations and identifying their immediate financial needs.

How we start this strategy sets the tone for the entire process. With your dedication and support, we will steer your child along the right path towards success. I truly believe that everyone has the potential to achieve their dreams and be whatever they want to be and do with time, dedication, and commitment. Each individual possesses unique talents waiting to be unlocked, and our role as parents or guardians is to guide them in their journey, so that success becomes attainable.

This first step is all about how much your child needs to earn and to establish their monetary or career aspirations for the future.

Exploring Career Options and Goals

Start by asking: What does your child really love to do? What is their passion or talent? We are all so unique and talented, it just takes some people longer to find their niche or talent.

I remember when my son Seb was a baby and all the mums would compare and work themselves up about the little details: That little Jimmy was crawling whereas Anne-Marie wasn't. Annabel was eating solids and Seb wouldn't even take a bottle. Although you might think your child is not "normal" – "Should I be worried?" – if all the health checks were okay and your child is happy and moving around, then who cares? It's their journey!

Everyone will grow and develop at different times and scales. The speed and degree of success your child achieves will hinge upon the support provided, the network they cultivate, and the research and dedication they invest in pursuing their career aspirations.

"Be yourself; everyone else is already taken."
– Oscar Wilde

What's your career goal? Is it mainly financial? At 21, I set my sights on earning an income, measured in thousands, that exceeded my age. I'll elaborate further in this chapter on an instance where I gained a crucial insight into salary. By the time I turned 30, my earnings were nearly twice my age. So it was fairly easy to negotiate my salary, as I knew what I wanted and how much I needed in relation to my age and financial goals.

That said, it's important to let your child know that it's okay not to know what you want to be at a younger age.

I didn't start doing what I truly love and feel I have a talent for until I was 40.

As we go through the steps, we will look a little more into how to deliver what your child wants to do and how to do it. But right now, it's about having an open conversation about what they think they want to do—now and in the future. It will take both of you to step out of your comfort zone, as their vision or passion may be something you don't understand or agree with. But do try to listen and be open to talk it through. This book will help guide you through that, and help you support decisions–or at the very least, to find resources to support.

Our Fears and Concerns About Our Child Getting Hired

Fear of making the wrong decision

You fear that you might guide your child down the wrong career path, leading to disappointment or regret in the future. This may stem from the pressure to provide accurate guidance or what your parents told or instilled in you when you were younger. The world has changed and will keep evolving, so it's best to stay agile, but supportive and go on the journey with them.

Concerns about financial stability

You worry about your child's ability to secure financially stable careers that can support their livelihood and aspirations. This is normal, but the following chapters will help alleviate or give you tools to help with this fear.

Uncertainty about future job markets

You may feel uncertain about the future job market and whether the career your child chooses will remain viable and in-demand. Artificial Intelligence (AI) is about to change the job market and I talk more about this in Chapter 3. You can only look at what's available now, as we will adapt and grow as new technology and job advancements change.

Desire for your child's happiness

Above all, you want your child to be happy and fulfilled in their chosen careers. The fear that children will end up in unfulfilling or unsatisfying jobs, or that they pick a wrong job despite your guidance and support is common. But we as parents will be there to support them nonetheless. I have certainly made a bad career move but I learnt a lot from it. We adapt and move on.

Pressure to meet societal expectations

You may feel pressured to steer your child towards careers that are perceived as prestigious or socially esteemed, even if those careers may not align with your child's interests or passions. This is also true of trying to get your child to follow in your or your family's footsteps, for example, as teachers, doctors, or lawyers. But we have to remember: Your child is not you, they may be unique and talented, but it's possible that their potential or talent does not truly align with the career you have chosen for them. Be supportive and open.

Fear of limited opportunities

You fear that your child may face limited opportunities or barriers in certain career fields due to factors such as gender, race, socioeconomic status, or geographic location. Again, remember that the world is different now; things may have changed for your child's circumstances, providing them endless possibilities. We just need to unlock and find the opportunity suitable for your child and their situation.

Worries about academic achievement

You may feel worried about your child's academic performance and how that may impact their career options. But there is so much support out there now, that there are opportunities for all and every ability.

Your child just needs to be committed to getting there. There is always a way if you or they want it enough.

Navigating these fears requires open communication, listening to what they want to do, a willingness to support, research and learn more to empower your child to succeed.

This book will help you navigate the fears and concerns that arise when supporting your child's career journey. Through open communication and a willingness to learn, you will gain the confidence to make informed decisions, ensuring your child's career path aligns with their interests and aspirations.

By embracing your child's individuality and developing a supportive environment, you can help your child achieve any role or career they want to pursue with confidence.

Research, Research, Research

The power of information and research cannot be overstated when it comes to guiding your child towards their desired career path. Understanding what your child wants to do requires thorough research into various industries, job roles, and educational pathways. Using a variety of tools and resources, leveraging online platforms like LinkedIn, Glassdoor, and professional networking events can provide valuable insights and connections to them.

By supporting and helping your child conduct comprehensive research, you enable them to navigate their career journey with confidence and clarity, ensuring that their choices align with their passions, skills, and aspirations. I will talk more about how to prompt, search and research in Chapter 3.

Setting and Understanding Financial Goals

I would advise parents to take a thoughtful approach when setting goals for your child. This process serves as a pivotal step in laying the groundwork for their future careers.

By setting clear expectations, such as talking them through the cost of living, you help them make more informed decisions and embark on their professional journeys with a sense of purpose and direction. Having open communication around these expectations is essential.

Establishing a supportive dialogue between you and your child ensures a mutual understanding of career goals, financial plans, and personal aspirations. This transparent communication becomes a foundation for a collaborative approach to navigating the next chapter in their life.

I would also highlight the importance of incorporating financial expectations into these discussions early. Teaching budgeting skills equips your child with the practical tools necessary for responsible financial management. Understanding income, expenses, and savings becomes an integral aspect of their journey toward a successful and sustainable professional life.

I am currently working with a parent whose child is comfortable on government benefits, and I believe it is holding him back from applying for more jobs as he has a safety net. Arnold Schwarzenegger says he never has a Plan B as it gives you an excuse to fail. It's interesting to put this into this context. If there is no safety net (government benefits), will it make your child more driven to get a job to support himself?

I wish budgeting was taught in schools as it would set the future generation up for more success. That's a whole new book! But a prime example of this was my first job after university. I was offered my dream job. I love rugby and had helped with a marketing event that offered us free tickets to Twickenham if we helped.

It was a no-brainer: a free trip to Twickenham! After the work we did and a few other events, I was offered a job in the centre of London. I was working with some of the biggest names in English Rugby at the time. I was organising black-tie events for a players' charity, getting free tickets to Rugby matches. Living the dream at 20!

However after travel, rent, buying dresses for events and food I worked out that I was actually losing money and getting into debt. My salary was so low. I didn't think or realise how much debt I was accruing. I had a student loan, so debt was normal. It was a steep learning curve.

Finally, my Dad sat me down one day and pointed out I was losing money every month and had to bail me out. I couldn't do it anymore. I was lucky to have the support of my Dad, and that I wasn't buried under thousands of pounds' worth of debt.

But students now are in so much debt it can become overwhelming. After this experience, I had more of an understanding of what salary I needed to earn to pay my bills, repay my Dad, and still have money to enjoy a few beers with my friends.

Together with your child, work out what options they should consider for what they want to do, and how much they should earn for it. Does your child need to contribute on a monthly basis, whether that's food, rent or both? The next generation doesn't often know how to budget, and your support with this early on can really help. It is often preferable to budget monthly rather than annually, as it can be challenging to comprehend large figures over a year. Monthly budgeting brings the financial plan into the present, and makes it more tangible and realistic.

In summary, my advice to parents is to invest the time and thoughtfulness needed to understand what you would like to do and set clear expectations for your child. This investment not only shapes their immediate decisions, but also equips them with the skills and mindset crucial for navigating the challenges and opportunities that lie ahead.

Coming Up With a Basic Plan

Now it's time to talk through options and choices with your child.

Typically, there are 3 choices after school, college or university:

1. Take a gap year;
2. Take up up further education; or
3. Take up paid work (including apprenticeships, internships and jobs).

What would *your* child like to do?

Why am I going to talk about gap years? If they want to work abroad, they may still need a CV, apply for and get the job/placement. If they want to progress to a master's degree, or other university course, they will still need to apply and interview for a place. The Six-Step Strategy can also be applied to all these scenarios.

Taking a Gap Year

Some questions you need to ask your child include:

- Where would you like to travel to? What would you like to see?
- How long would you want to go for?
- Who would you go with?

Gap years are not a bad thing; they are great to read for HR or hiring managers, as it means that the individual has travelled and has managed to learn, see and experience different cultures and peoples. It is a positive thing to read on a CV. Getting paid work experience whilst travelling is even better, as you can now do both.

I went travelling on my own at the age of 29, and it was amazing! I met people who travelled in pairs or groups, and they really struggled, as not everyone agreed on the next destination or activity. If your child is travelling with a group, make sure that they talk about what they would like to do and see in each country, so that expectations are clear.

The reason I went travelling so late is that I got a job and stayed in the same town after university as many friends did. We all stayed for a few years, before I moved with my then-partner, who was a professional rugby player. When the relationship ended and I left my role, it was just perfect timing to take stock, explore the world, and experience new things.

Travelling at 29 meant I had more money and didn't have to work. I enjoyed the experience. Travelling is never frowned upon unless…you disclose you want to go travelling whilst applying for a permanent job, and not a temporary role. (It's important we emphasise to our children to act with integrity).

What are the benefits of your child going travelling?

Personal growth and self-discovery
Travelling will expose your child to new cultures, perspectives, and ways of life, helping them gain a broader understanding of the world and their place in it. Navigating unfamiliar situations and overcoming challenges while travelling can boost your child's self-confidence, problem-solving skills, and independence.

Experiencing different cultures and ways of life can help your child develop empathy, tolerance, and open-mindedness
Travelling can be an extension of classroom learning, providing hands-on experiences that reinforce academic concepts in subjects like history, geography, and cultural studies. Interacting with locals and immersing themselves in a new culture can be a valuable language-learning experience, especially for those studying a foreign language.

I have fond memories of visiting schools, going fishing with the locals and helping where I could. I met an accountant from Somerset and we went to visit a school and the young children all sang the wheels on the bus and practised their English. I will never forget the joy I felt when we clapped and sang along with them.

Volunteering or interning abroad can give your child practical experience in their field of interest and help them develop professional skills. Travelling can help your child discover new interests and passions, which can inform their career choices and lead to more fulfilling work.

Travelling with friends or family can strengthen relationships and create lasting memories. Meeting new people from different backgrounds while travelling can lead to lifelong friendships and professional connections. I am still connected to the people I travelled with 20 years ago. Michelle, who I met in Miami, actually got a pack of playing cards and wrote everyone she met on a separate card (I think I was the 7 of spades) her travels and when she finished laid them out and tagged us all in. We all shared great memories of missing flights, South Beach, eating alligator and getting attacked by seagulls.

Exploring the world shows them new cultures and ways of life opening their eyes to the incredible diversity of our world. By immersing themselves in these unfamiliar environments, they will gain a deeper understanding and appreciation for how others live. Your child will learn to see the world through fresh eyes, developing a more global and compassionate mindset.

This broadening of horizons can have a profound impact, inspiring them to learn and grow in exciting new ways.

Travelling has the power to transform young people, opening their minds, expanding their perspectives, and setting them on inspiring new paths of discovery and personal growth. The experiences they have and the people they meet will stay with them forever, shaping who they become.

By encouraging your child to travel, you are giving them the opportunity to grow, learn, and discover in ways that will benefit them personally, academically, and professionally throughout their life.

If your child is considering travelling, advise them to seek more temporary employment, particularly those in larger corporations or in the retail sector. These companies often offer more flexible contracts due to their extensive workforce, placing value on overtime and flexibility.

As a senior manager in larger retail corporations, I wanted to support my staff whether they wanted to join the police force, the fire service, or to go travelling. If your child wants to go travelling, they can consider jobs with extra scope for overtime to boost the bank balance before they go. Senior leaders loved this type of employee as they would carry out huge amounts of overtime for travel money. They work to earn, then travel; they come back, earn again, and go off again.

This is also true of University students, as we were able to transfer them to different sites and stores. They worked for one store during term time, and another one on holidays. It was the perfect scenario for both employer and employee.

Taking Up Further Education

University graduates I speak to sometimes want to get all the studying out the way before they go to work. In their words, it was "putting off becoming an adult and getting a job."

This is not a bad decision. Having personally completed academic learning 20 years after graduating, I had a hard time getting back to writing in the third party and Harvard Referencing.

One thing to consider if your child is looking at continuing their studies, is if they have an idea of a career they would like to go into, are there "feeder" universities for the career or job roles your child wants to do? By going to University or taking up a Master's degree at this feeder* University, they extend their network (i.e. alumni), creating more opportunities for them.

A "feeder" university is an educational institution known for consistently producing graduates highly sought after by specific industries or employers.

These universities serve as prime sources or pipelines for talented individuals in particular fields due to their high-quality education, specialised programs, and industry-focused curricula. Employers often target feeder universities because graduates are well-prepared and possess the desired expertise or knowledge in their respective fields.

As a result, these institutions serve as reliable sources of talent for organisations seeking highly qualified and industry-relevant professionals, emphasising their pivotal role in fulfilling staffing needs.

You can do a bit of research on LinkedIn about staff that have been hired from each University by looking at the analytics on a company. LinkedIn and its opportunities will be discussed more in Chapter 5.

Taking Up Paid Work

The benefits of going straight into work offers a lot of opportunities to travel later on, or even pick up academic qualifications and certifications paid for by employers.

There are many government initiatives out there to support this. Your child just needs to know what area or industry they would like to work in. And as advised above, research to get the details and make an informed decision.

Some schools put a lot of emphasis on going to University, but with fees and cost of living it is not for everyone and not everyone can afford it. I personally loved it but didn't have to pay the fees there are now. The pandemic also opened up so many more opportunities to study and learn remotely.

Exercise 1

After talking to your child, what would they like to do? (If they are not sure yet, keep going. This book will help, and by Step 3 they will be able to…) Tick one:

- ☐ Take a gap year or go travelling
- ☐ Take up further education
- ☐ Take on a paid job

How much do they need to earn per month?

£

Here's where they can dream big:

What would they REALLY love to do or earn monthly?

Chapter 2
Step 2: Keyword Searches and Research

"The future belongs to those who believe in the beauty of their dreams." – Eleanor Roosevelt

In this chapter, I will show you the power of having the right information and doing targeted research in your child's career exploration.

I will also talk a lot about keywords.

Keywords Are King

Keywords are indispensable tools in the process of gaining employment–from refining job searches to crafting compelling applications and securing interviews. These strategic terms serve as the linchpin in optimising CVs, cover letters, and online profiles to align with employer preferences and job requirements.

When searching for roles, particularly online, using industry-specific keywords ensures that job seekers uncover relevant opportunities tailored to their skillset and their career aspirations.

In the competitive landscape of job applications, on the other hand, strategically embedding keywords into CVs and application letters showcase an individual's suitability for the role, effectively communicating their qualifications and experiences that hirers are seeking.

Keywords play a crucial role in job searching as they represent the core aspects of the job seeker's preferences, qualifications, and priorities. When selecting keywords, such as "graduate," "salary," and "location," job seekers can effectively filter through job listings to find opportunities that align with their specific criteria.

"Graduate" indicates that the job seeker is seeking positions suitable for recent graduates or individuals with entry-level experience. This keyword helps narrow down the search to roles that offer opportunities for career growth and development.

"Salary" signifies what your child knows or wants to earn (see Chapter 1). Select or type this in a keyword search field as it will also differentiate results that come up. The higher the salary, the higher the technical or experience level required.

"Location" denotes the geographic preference of your child. Whether it's a specific city, region, or remote work option, including this keyword ensures that job seekers find opportunities in their desired locations, reducing the need for extensive commuting or relocation.

This strategic approach can also be applied to future career transitions. I use this when I coach and mentor managers or executives. We often deploy more refined keywords tailored to their specific requirements, or what we call "role-specific keywords." An example would be "agile projects" or certain certifications or qualifications, like Prince2® or Network+.

However, the fundamental principle remains the same: Utilise strategic keywords to refine job searches and target opportunities aligned with your child's career goals. Mastering the art of keyword selection is essential for navigating the job market effectively.

Similarly, refining your key word prompts can give you vastly different outcomes.

I stress the importance of this as I always find roles that suit my clients that they haven't found. If I had £1 for every time I got a message like, "I didn't see that role," or "How did you find that job? It's perfect!" It all boils down to using strategically simple keywords.

Finding keywords that really embody what your child wants to do will help them hone in on jobs that matter to them.

Timing Is of the Essence

Additionally, selecting job postings within a specific timeframe, such as within seven days, ensures that job seekers are viewing the most recent and relevant listings.

This approach helps job seekers stay updated on new opportunities and increases their chances of finding openings before they become oversaturated with applicants.

When I help my HR consultancy clients recruit, I always say prime talent is hired within 10 days, so be prepared to move quickly. I will talk more about this later in Chapter 6: Job Application Management and Support

For now, search roles that have been posted within seven days, as this also stops the algorithm from making you look at the same jobs over and over.

In summary, by strategically selecting keywords and filtering job postings based on chronology, your child can streamline their job search process, focus on relevant opportunities, and increase their chances of finding the perfect job match.

Refining Your Search

Once you have established some keywords, pop them into a search tool, AI or a job platform. Only use 3 words at a time, and do not type in a job title–unless it's a really niche role.

Let's take HR as an example.

There are more than 17 different roles within HR, and every company uses something different:

HR Generalist, HR Manager, HR Coordinator, HR Specialist, HR Director, HR Administrator, HR Assistant, HR Consultant, HR Business Partner, HR

Analyst, HR Recruiter, HR Advisor, HR Executive, HR Officer, HR Intern, HR Payroll Specialist, HR Lead, and many more.

Some even use People instead of HR, as in People Partners, People and Culture Lead. So instead of using a job title, advise your child to think about what they would like to do in that role.

Maximising Academic Support

As parents, it's important to encourage your child to utilise the resources and support available to them through their school, college, or university that may help them navigate their career options. These educational institutions offer a wide range of opportunities aimed at assisting students in finding suitable employment opportunities that align with their interests and goals.

One of the first steps parents can take is to encourage their child to engage with their school's career services department or guidance counsellors early in their studies. These professionals are equipped to provide valuable guidance and assistance into what career options are available to them, and advise on support or events that could help them explore these options.

Additionally, parents can encourage their child to participate in events organised by the school, such as job fairs, career workshops, and networking events. These activities provide invaluable opportunities for students to interact with potential employers, learn about job openings, and gain insights into various industries and job roles.

It's essential for parents to emphasise the importance of exploring diverse career options and keeping an open mind during this process. Encouraging your child to explore different industries and job roles can help them discover their passions and strengths, ultimately leading to a more fulfilling career path.

By actively engaging with their school, college, or university and taking advantage of the resources and support available, you can help your child make informed decisions about their future and set them on the path to success.

Exercise 2

Robin Sharna says "Dream big, start small, act now."

Pick the 3 keywords that you and your child are going to search.

1. _____
2. _____
3. _____

Don't feel pressured to rush into deciding what career is right for your child now. It's okay if your child is unsure about what they want to do at the moment. Take action by helping them explore different options, and seeing what opportunities come their way.

If they're still uncertain, that's alright too. Let them know that they can always revisit their career aspirations once they have a clearer idea or stronger options to consider whilst moving through the steps.

AI technology can be a valuable tool to assist them in their search. There are options to complete career quizzes or research to support searching opportunities in the area your child wants to work in.

In the next chapter, we'll explore how AI can provide you with a significant advantage by streamlining the process of searching, writing, and applying for jobs, planning gap years, or selecting universities. This technology can make your journey much smoother and more efficient, giving you the edge you need to succeed.

"Artificial intelligence is probably the most important thing humanity has ever worked on. I think of it as something that will be transformative."

– Sundar Pichai, CEO of Google

Chapter 3
Use Artificial Intelligence as a Powerful Resource

"Artificial intelligence is not a substitute for human intelligence; it is a tool to amplify human creativity and ingenuity. " – Fei-Fei Li

We are offered thousands of resources throughout our careers and our lives, but what guarantees our success is how resourceful we are with these tools. This chapter is dedicated to how the world is changing with AI, love it or hate it, it's not going away, and how our children can use it as a means of finding career fulfilment.

Insights show that in the next five years AI will replace 85 million existing jobs. However, it will also create 97 million jobs, 80% of which haven't even been invented yet, and will generate $15.7 trillion.[1]

So how can you maximise it?

This chapter offers you, as parents, a basic guide to understanding AI, its responsible use in the context as a tool to help save time and to maximise your child's job applications. We will also address the potential risks associated with AI, and underline the necessity of implementing ethical controls to ensure responsible utilisation.

Engaging in a conversation with your child about the evolution of job searching is crucial. Reflect on the differences between your job-seeking experience compared to the modern day, emphasising the rapid changes over the past five years. Encourage your child to stay informed, to embrace adaptability, and to proactively prepare for the future.

Basic Guide to AI for Parents
What is Artificial Intelligence?
AI refers to the development of computer systems and software that can perform tasks typically requiring human intelligence. It encompasses various techniques, including machine learning, natural language processing, robotics, and computer vision.

What is the Difference Between AI and Google?

Google is a company that provides a search engine to find relevant information, while AI is a broader field that encompasses technologies mentioned above, all of which are used in various industries and domains.

AI tools that are already in common use include ChatGPT and Perplexity, both of which are being used for various purposes, such as education and entertainment.

However, as a parent, it's important to understand and to communicate to our children that while AI can be helpful, it's not a replacement for human interaction and guidance.

How Does AI Learn?

AI learns through data-driven processes. In machine learning, AI models are trained on data, adjusting their parameters to make predictions or decisions. Reinforcement learning uses feedback from interactions with an environment to improve over time.

An example of this is data collection. AI can collect vast amounts of data from past customer interactions and websites. This data includes variables such as browsing history, items viewed, time spent on each page, purchase history, demographic, information etc.

What are the Different Types of AI?

AI can be categorised into three main types: Narrow AI (Weak AI) designed for specific tasks, General AI (Strong AI) with human-like intelligence, and Artificial Superintelligence (ASI) surpassing the limitations of human intelligence.

What are the Common Ways AI is Being Used?

AI is surprising us with unexpected and innovative solutions, from pollinating crops using tiny robots to creating breakthrough technologies in legal research and process automation.

AI-powered virtual assistants like Siri, Alexa, and Google Assistant provide personalised support and perform tasks based on voice commands, such as setting reminders, answering questions, and controlling smart home devices. A lot of businesses are already using this for marketing and basic administrative tasks.

What are the Most Frequently Used AI Platforms?

When it comes to which AI platforms are more popular, it boils down, it seems, to personal preference, a bit like Apple VS. Android.

I myself use ChaptGPT and Perplexity in most of the work that I do. I personally find ChatGPT the best at rewriting sentences and paragraphs, while Perplexity is great for research, as it brings up website sources immediately (in ChatGPT, you need to prompt it to do that). As an alternative, Google has Bard.

The Risks of Using AI

Whilst I love AI and use it daily, I am cautious about the increasing influence of AI on our daily lives. Here are some common concerns you and your child should be aware of, so both of you can be mindful of your use of this new technology, in the same way we have been when other new technologies like mobile phones and social media were introduced to us in the past.

1. **Lack of transparency**

   AI systems can sometimes make decisions that people don't understand, which may lead to unexpected outcomes.

2. **Bias and discrimination**

   AI algorithms can sometimes be biased, leading to unfair treatment of certain groups of people.

3. **Privacy concerns**

   The use of AI can raise concerns about the privacy of personal data and how it is used.

4. **Ethical dilemmas**

   AI raises complex ethical questions, some of which may impact job displacement.

5. **Security risks**

   As AI technologies become more advanced, the potential for misuse and security breaches also increases.

As the world continues to be shaped by the rise of AI, it is essential for parents to recognise the transformative potential of this technology, and to be mindful of using it in an ethical and controlled way.

While AI is set to disrupt *and* create millions of jobs, it is crucial to understand that success in the future will depend on how resourceful individuals are in utilising the available tools and resources.

By using AI responsibly for your child's career development, parents can influence and enhance their child's employability and provide better job search outcomes. By being aware of the risks of AI, you can check, revise and guide your child in the ever-changing landscape of job-hunting.

Using AI for Application Management Support

One of the most straightforward approaches to utilising AI in the job search process is through application management support.

By prompting AI to research jobs, industries, and market trends in your area or county, you can gain insights into available career opportunities for your children. Simply ask AI questions like, "What jobs are available based on my child's interests in [brand, hobbies, industry, town, county?" This initiates AI's search for relevant job postings, providing valuable information on potential career paths.

Using AI to Help Your Child Get Hired

There are a multitude of ethically sound ways one can use AI to help your child find the right career for them. One is by thinking of AI as a junior career assistant. AI can:

- Help generate essential keywords,
- Write compelling CVs,
- Produce professionally written cover letters,
- Carry out research on prospective companies, and
- Ultimately help increase their chances of getting hired.

AI can even check for typos and mistakes, if given the correct prompts! So how does this work in practice?

Tailoring CVs

Utilise AI as a CV-writing resource. It used to take me hours to write CVs for people, which is why some people used to charge £100s to write CVs. But in my opinion, 1 CV does not fit all roles. It must be tailored to each job and company. I would use AI to tailor your CV for specific roles, as many recruiters and hiring managers rely on automated applicant tracking systems called ATS. This uses AI to filter job seekers' CVs in seconds, significantly reducing the time recruiters spend reviewing CVs. Using AI effectively can help ensure your CV aligns with the job requirements and gets through this screening by matching key words.

Producing cover letters

AI can help generate well-structured and tailored cover letters, enhancing your chances for interview and employment.

Undertaking research

AI (along with company websites) can be used to research the company's understanding, missions, vision and values, and ask what examples or types of questions you may get asked for this job role.

By incorporating these AI-driven strategies into your job search, your child can enhance their employability with a business or company they align with.

I will be mentioning AI throughout this book, as it will significantly help your child save time, and aid their application process to get hired. I urge you to have a play on AI to help with your job search and application support. It used to take me hours to write CVs, cover letters, and do interview prep for other people. Now, as I use AI every day, all those tasks now take me minutes. Whilst cautious, I understand that AI is a resource that will give any job-seeker a competitive edge.

Using AI to Undertake Job Assessments

If your child is not sure what you would like to do as a career or job, use AI to search for FREE career quizzes or type in keywords or phrases that reveal jobs matching their skills, hobbies and interests. Try keywords such as brands you like, the town you live in, hobbies, clubs or academic courses that they have just completed.

Type in these prompts *"What FREE career quizzes are there for graduates that don't know what to do after studying in the UK"*

Refinement and Personalisation Through Keyword Optimisation

Parents can teach their child to further leverage AI by extracting keywords from specific job advertisements. They can instruct AI to find a job, copy the job description, and identify the keywords. By then inputting their child's CV into the AI and asking it to compare against the keywords, parents can ensure that the CV aligns with the requirements of the job. This step streamlines the process of tailoring the CV to specific job roles, increasing the chances of catching the employer's attention.

I have added some bonus prompts at the end of the chapter to maximise AI.

Interview Preparation

Your child can use AI to understand what the missions, vision and values of the company they are keen to join are. This can simply be done by prompting, for example:

"Tell me everything you know about [name of company] which I am looking at applying for the role of [job position]."

Additional preparation for job interviews can be done by analysing job adverts and predicting potential interview questions. It is possible to input job adverts into AI and ask it to generate typical interview questions for the respective roles. This can help your children anticipate and prepare for interviews more effectively, boosting their confidence and performance during the hiring process.

Whilst this kind of preparation can give them confidence going into interviews, AI will never be 100% accurate. Still, it gives them an idea of what to expect, which significantly improves their preparedness. I will cover more on this topic in Chapter 7.

Preparing for an interview can simply be done by prompting AI:

"What questions may be asked for an interview for this job role?"

"What would be good answers for these questions?"

Note that these are just supposed to be a guide for your child, but if they tend to be nervous, being this prepared will help practise them for their interview.

Summarising the Use of AI

Embracing AI as a junior assistant in your child's job search and application journey can significantly enhance their prospects.

By using AI for application management, keyword optimisation, CV and cover letter refinement, as well as interview preparation, you can equip your child with the tools needed to pursue their career aspirations with the right tools and support.

It's crucial to remember that AI tools are not the sole source of information for your child. Encouraging human interaction can aid in deepening their understanding of the material. Additionally, it's important to remind them that they are interacting with each other. This balanced approach, where AI complements human judgement, is key to achieving success in their searches and applications.

I will finish this chapter with top AI prompts, but remember to act with integrity at all times!

Take point 7 as an example. Whilst it will offer suggestions, if your child does not have these skills, certifications, or qualifications, DO NOT ENCOURAGE THEM TO LIE!

I remember talking to a friend whose mum said she was an expert in Excel. When she got the job, she didn't have a clue what she was doing and was let go very quickly. Do not let this happen to your child

Top 10 AI Prompts for Creating, Adapting, and Improving a CV:

1. "Generate a professional summary for my CV based on my career goals and key skills." [prompt goal, skills, certifications]

2. "Identify and extract keywords from a specific job description [job advert] to tailor my CV accordingly."

3. "Review my CV for spelling and grammar errors, and suggest corrections."

4. "Provide feedback on the layout and design of my CV to enhance readability and visual appeal."

5. "Rewrite my bullet points to make them more outcome-focused and impactful."

6. "Suggest action verbs to start each bullet point in my work experience section."

7. "Recommend additional skills or qualifications to include in my CV based on industry trends."

8. "Create a customised cover letter template that complements my CV for a specific job [Job advert] application."

9. "Optimise my CV for applicant tracking systems (ATS) by ensuring it contains relevant keywords."

10. "Offer insights on how to quantify my achievements and experiences to strengthen my CV's impact."

Exercise 3

With your child, create an account with their preferred AI tool (such as ChatGPT or Bard) and start playing with some prompts. You can also upload your child's CV and see how else it can be improved (truthfully, ethically).

"Your CV is your personal advertisement, so make it a powerful selling tool."

– Judith Johnstone

Chapter 4
Step 3: Crafting a Standout CV

"Knowledge isn't power until it is applied."
– Dale Carnegie

This chapter is all about how vitally important crafting a CV is to get your child an interview, and ultimately get hired.

A well-crafted CV is not merely a list of qualifications and experiences but a powerful tool that showcases a candidate's unique talents, skills, and potential to prospective employers. It serves as the first impression, capturing the attention of recruiters and setting the stage for further consideration.

This chapter will offer guidance to assist your child in crafting compelling CVs. With attention to detail, strategic language, and alignment with industry expectations, a well-crafted CV becomes the key that unlocks for your child countless opportunities for success in the competitive job market.

With over two decades of experience in CV writing, I've dedicated myself to supporting graduates, colleagues, peers, supervisors, managers, executives and regional directors in writing impactful CVs. As a career strategist, I've witnessed firsthand the transformative power of a well-written CV.

With some tweaks and guidance to their CVs, I have taken people I have coached and mentored from getting zero interviews to being invited to ALL interviews they apply for, and eventually leading to job offers—all thanks to basic changes in their CVs. That only goes to show that this vital document serves as your child's pathway to new opportunities, showcasing an individual's talents and experiences in a compelling manner.

In today's competitive job market, understanding the importance of an accurately tailored CV is paramount to your child's career success.

While the future may bring innovations, like digital applications or video reels, the fundamental principle remains unchanged: Match your CV to the job advertisement. Understanding what the employer is seeking and aligning your qualifications and experiences accordingly is crucial.

Whether it's through a traditionally written CV or emerging formats like video presentations, the key is to effectively communicate how your skills and achievements meet the specific requirements outlined in the job advertisement. By doing so, you increase your chances of standing out as a qualified candidate and securing opportunities in today's competitive job market.

Here are some hard-hitting statistics that show why we need to get your CV accurate and effective. In a study conducted by the New College of Humanities and published in an article on *Good Housekeeping UK*[2], they found these top reasons why CVs are rejected by potential employers:

1. Typos and grammatical errors (59%)
2. Overly casual tone (50%)
3. Use of jargon and clichés (50%), i.e. "thinking outside the box"
4. A CV more than two pages long (47%)

5. Snazzy borders and backgrounds (44%)
6. Writing in the third person (43%)
7. Inclusion of clip art or emojis (42%)
8. Use of cringeworthy quotes (39%)
9. Unprofessional email address (32%)
10. Unconventional font (31%)

Creating a Master CV

The first thing I always suggest is to create a Master CV. This document contains all your professional experience, skills, and qualifications, serving as a comprehensive record of your career. This should ideally be updated throughout your career.

Having a master CV will allow you to tailor specific CVs for different job applications by selecting, copying, and pasting the most relevant information for each role. This approach ensures that each CV is customised for the role you are applying for, making the application process more efficient and effective.

The reason your CV needs to be so specific and tailored to the role is twofold:

1. If you do not match keywords it will be rejected if ATS* is being used.
2. HR or Line Managers often spend a mere 7 seconds reviewing a CV.

The software commonly known as an "Applicant Tracking System" (ATS) automates the processing of job applications, allowing recruiters to filter and organise CVs based on specific criteria (skills, experience, and qualifications), using algorithms to identify keywords and match them to the job requirements. This enables efficient management of large application volumes and focuses on the most relevant candidate.

It is imperative that your child's CV captures attention swiftly and effectively, maximising the chances of progressing through the initial stages of the selection process. You also want your first few lines to be engaging and want the reader to read more. It's the same principle as with most adverts and promotional material: If it doesn't grab your attention, you just tend to scroll on.

The attention your child needs to create should be one for accuracy and a great match for a role, rather than a cheesy over-the-top statement like "I am the candidate for you, look no further." And by the way, I *have* read a CV that stated that. In my opinion there is a fine line between confidence ("I have the skills for the role and I am a good match") and arrogance ("I am your dream candidate").

Including your postcode is crucial because ATS and recruitment databases often use postcodes to search for candidates. Companies and recruiters consider factors like travel time to and from work, assessing if it's feasible for someone to commute for an hour or rely on public transport.

If you're applying for positions outside your current area, it's essential to emphasise your willingness to relocate and your ability to do so within a four-week timeframe if offered the job.

Additionally, if you live in a rural area, mentioning that you have access to a car and can drive to work can be beneficial.

Tailoring Your Child's CV to the Role

When I coach and mentor my clients I liken a CV to picking or buying a car, a mobile phone, or a house. You have a list of things you want and need when buying any of these major items i.e. "The house must have a garden, 3 bathrooms and 4 bedrooms."

This is no different to the candidate that must have at least one-year experience in customer service or a Maths GCSE. If you were looking for a 2-bathroom house and it only has one, but has a downstairs toilet, this would be a compromise. Which is why you see written on adverts the words "required," "desired," or "relevant experience," as in:

- Customer service experience required/desired
- Degree in Marketing (or relevant experience)

I was talking to a client who was considering a Marketing role, but didn't have a degree, so he said he wouldn't apply for it. But he had run his own events company for seven years. This counts as relevant experience, as he had to market the events in order for them to be successful.

This is where practical experience rather than academic knowledge/study can also be used to your child's advantage. Some employers prefer experience over academics, as they themselves may not have gone to University.

An interesting fact about the difference between women and men at this point is that women tend to only apply if they believe that they match 100% of the criteria, whereas men only have to match 60%. So why do women doubt their abilities more than men?

Many women believe the hiring process is purely based on meeting all the listed qualifications, rather than understanding that advocacy, relationships, and framing of the expertise can help overcome not having every single qualification. Parents, your daughters may need more help and persuasion to apply for certain roles!

A prime example of this is when I was hosting a workshop at a college, and a lecturer and I were carrying out mock interviews. I said to the students, "Detail your hobbies if you don't have huge amounts of work experience. Playing sport, for example, shows teamwork, commitment, and dedication."

The lecturer came back after mock interviewing his student and said that whilst interviewing her, he found out she was a junior world champion horse rider, but hadn't put it in her CV. Why? She came 2nd that year! Generally speaking, women need more confidence and be comfortable with being able to show their experience.

Going back to the house analogy: If a house in a listing didn't have some of your "must-haves," you would immediately rule it out. But if you see a few options that have some of the requirements on your list, you would proceed with a viewing or would request more details from the seller.

How many viewings do you often go to before you find the right house?

It's the same for recruitment. An initial call is a "find out more about you"; the 1st interview = first viewing, and 2nd interview may be a technical presentation, or the 2nd viewing of a house to really look into nook and cranny to ensure it's the right move.

For students who haven't bought a house or car, you could use the mobile phone buying analogy. What type of phone are you looking for? Apple? Android? How big do you want it to be? Are you interested in certain specifications? What capacity does it need? 32GB or

64GB? What colour are you looking for—silver, black, rose gold? Relate this scenario so your child understands the process.

These specifications and want list are the same as the job advert; this is what the recruiter is looking for. This is what they want and need, just like how you rejected a house that didn't have everything you needed. It's the same for applying for jobs; if it doesn't have something that was imperative for your list, you reject it. If it did have something similar or that could work, you requested more information and explained the relevance or compromise to the listing. So it's important that your child showcases the relevant experience rather than the certification.

Think of your child's CV as you would want to see your house promoted for sale via an estate agent, with the best photographs possible and the rooms being neat and clutter free, to ensure you have the best chance of securing maximum viewing and the best possible sale price. A well-written and well-presented CV is there to achieve the same goal, which is to create that very positive first impression, to secure the interview, and to lead to a job offer and a start date.

What Should the CV Contain?

Personal Information

The foundation of any CV is personal information. Check that your child includes their full name, first name, surname, town, and county (though do note they don't have to write their full address), contact details, and a professionally oriented email address.

This establishes the initial connection between the applicant and the prospective employer.

Detailing a mobile phone number that works sounds obvious but, in my career, I have rejected 20-30% of candidates as I couldn't get hold of them an out-of-date or incorrect mobile number usually being the reason.

Personal Statement

The personal statement in a CV, similar to an executive summary in a business plan or report, briefly introduces the applicant, their key strengths, their interest in the role they are applying for, and their desire to work for the company they are applying to.

It serves as a concise overview of their professional identity and career goals, aiming to capture the attention of potential employers and convey their fit for the position and organisation. Employers and HR will always read this and it's a good opportunity to get some key words in.

This is the advert hook for the recruiter to want to read: "Are you what we need?"

Below is an example for a marketing position:
I am an enthusiastic and dedicated marketing professional with a proven track record of creating and implementing successful marketing strategies. With strong analytical skills and a creative mindset, I thrive in fast-paced environments and enjoy working as part of a dynamic team. I am now seeking a challenging role as a [Job Title] in a forward-thinking company like [Company] where I can contribute my skills to drive impactful marketing campaigns and achieve mutual success.

If your child has no work experience yet, they can write something like this:
As a recent graduate with a strong foundation in marketing, I am eager to apply my analytical skills and creative mindset to a challenging role [or detail the job title] within a forward-thinking company like [Company]. I have a proven track record of developing and implementing successful marketing strategies,

and I thrive in fast-paced, collaborative environments.
I am enthusiastic about the opportunity to contribute
to impactful marketing campaigns and achieve mutual
success in a dynamic professional setting.

Key Skills

Beyond academic qualifications, the skills section is an opportunity to showcase a diverse range of competencies. Whether it's effective communication, teamwork, or technical proficiency, this segment allows your child to match the keywords they need and showcase their strengths.

What are they good at, what do they enjoy doing? Let them have a look at the list below, they must feel confident talking about themselves, whether that's applying for a job for a gap year, or interviewing for a master's degree where they need to support themselves.

These are really important if they don't have any previous jobs and are leaving college or university. Take a look at some examples below.

Top soft skills that employers are looking for in graduates include:

1. **Time Management**

   The ability to use time efficiently and work effectively

2. **Communication**

   Strong verbal and written communication skills

3. **Adaptability**

   Being flexible and adaptable to change (for example the Covid-19 pandemic significantly changed how one studied)

4. **Problem-Solving**

   The capability to identify and resolve problems using critical thinking and analysis

5. **Teamwork**

   Ability to work effectively in a team, share responsibility, and respect others' input

6. **Creativity**

   Thinking creatively to develop new ideas and solutions

7. **Leadership**

   Demonstrating leadership qualities, such as motivating a team and resolving conflicts (School prefect, head of year, school counsellor, captain, vice-captain of sport, scout leader, brownies, guides, games master)

8. **Interpersonal Skills**

   Building strong working relationships and resolving conflicts (Have you got lots of friends? Do you stop the arguments within your friends?)

9. **Work Ethic**

   Having a strong sense of responsibility and a dedicated work approach (Do you stick at things and like to see them through?)

10. **Attention to Detail**

    Being thorough and accurate in task completion (Ability to use spell check, grammar, and AI)

These soft skills are highly valued by employers and can significantly enhance your child's ability to get hired for various roles. Don't overthink these and as a parent help support or reinforce your child's strengths and give them confidence.

If your child has skills such as team development and management, enhancing guest or customer experiences, and impacting the bottom line positively, it's essential to showcase these abilities. Recommend to them to highlight instances where they've demonstrated leadership in developing and growing teams, or ensuring satisfaction and loyalty in customer interactions, and contributing to the overall success of projects or initiatives. These skills significantly enhance their appeal to potential employers.

Professional Achievements or Certifications

Every achievement, be it academic or extracurricular, contributes to the full picture of the candidate. This section is a platform to showcase noteworthy accomplishments, emphasising the candidate's dedication and potential.

Education

The education section serves as a record of your child's academic achievements. Include details of academic qualifications and ongoing studies, showcasing the commitment to learning and development.

The main results most employers look for are Maths and English, don't worry if they haven't got loads of qualifications and certifications. Degrees don't hold the same weight they used to, and every company is looking for something different.

Scoring and grading in education has changed over the years, we are used to letter grades but many are now numerical. If your child is part of academia and their future career is very dependent on their qualifications, list each subject especially if they scored 9/A* equivalent promote your academia.

If they are an average student *like I was* – put 7 GCSE grades 1-5 and list them as examples and avoid detailing very low scores.

See detail below of examples.

Example 1

Dates 2015 – 2019

| School Name | **3 GCSE Grade 9** | English, double science |
| | **7 GCSE Grade 5-8** | Maths, Drama etc |

Example 2 (me)

Dates 2015-2019

| School Name | **7 GCSEs Grades 5-9** | English, Maths, Science, etc. |

Work Experience or History

Highlighting relevant work experience is important in showing competence and practical applications of skills. This section should include part-time jobs, work experience, internships, volunteer work, and even events organised by schools (like helping with shows, sports events, and end-of-year proms). These productions provide a glimpse into what the candidate has done previously.

Make sure to consistently highlight key responsibilities and achievements in your work experience section. Don't assume that employers will automatically understand the specifics of your previous roles. For instance, if you worked at a major chain retailer, specify whether it was a Superstore, Mega store or Convenience store. Provide details such as the size of your team, the training you received, and the metrics by which your performance was evaluated. This clarity will give potential employers a better understanding of your background and skills.

Even a week's work experience is worth putting on their CV. They just need to put the year they did it and detail what they did. What soft skills did they use from the above list? Did they serve or talk to customers? What were their responsibilities?

In this section if they have had a job, it will have a job description. Use the bullet points from their offer letter or contract to detail what they did in that role.

Emphasising the importance of including detailed information about previous roles in your child's CV is crucial. This not only provides a comprehensive overview of their professional, or even work experience or previous jobs but also allows potential employers to quickly understand the measurable impact and successes they've achieved

For instance, instead of generic statements, encourage your child to express growth more effectively. For example, they could highlight their leadership by stating, "I was part of a team team that achieved an impressive 10% year-on-year sales growth" or showcase their exceptional performance with, "I exceeded or helped deliver sales targets by £20,000 in a pivotal project, demonstrating proficiency in meeting key performance indicators (KPIs)."

In essence, incorporating specific metrics like percentages or monetary figures transforms the CV into a powerful tool, enabling your child to communicate their achievements in a way that resonates with hiring managers and enhances their chances in the competitive job market.

For graduates just starting out it could be as simple as "I helped raise £3,000 for [Charity] by organising a charity fun run by promoting it in the local community and on social media" or "I helped grow the annual [Charity] fun run by 15% by promoting it in the local community and on social media."

These are the kinds of statements that HR, recruiters or managers (and even the ATS) will be looking for, so it's important to ensure that your child's CV showcases these.

Hobbies

While many recruiters may advise against including hobbies on a CV, I firmly believe it is crucial to showcase activities your child enjoys, such as gaming, walking, or socialising. These interests, ideally mainstream, can provide valuable talking points during an interview. For instance, mentioning support for a particular football team may strike a chord with a potential employer, who shares the same allegiance or supports an opposing team. Similarly, being a member of a scout's group could create a connection if your interviewer's son was also a scout.

When companies advertise a job, they seek individuals who not only add value and commit for an extended period, but also contribute to the growth of their business. Highlighting shared interests or commonalities within the team can be a significant advantage in this regard. This approach shows the importance of including personal interests in a CV to establish connections and create engaging talking points during the interview process.

When including sports in your child's CV, make sure to provide specific details such as the sports played, the level of participation, and any relevant affiliations. For example, mention playing golf at a particular club and specify your handicap, or highlight being part of the first XI cricket or hockey team for a specific club. It's important to provide concrete information rather than just listing generic sports like golf, cricket, or horse riding.

References

If your child intends to leave school, college, or university, it is advisable to obtain as many recommendations and references as they can. They can approach their tutors for these, ideally selecting those who like them and will give them a glowing reference, or provide a strong endorsement. These endorsements can be valuable additions to their LinkedIn profile as well as their CV.

While requesting feedback can be challenging, the reinforcement or confidence and support of their abilities and contributions can be immensely rewarding. It can also set them apart from other candidates, particularly when they lack extensive work experience.

It is important to emphasise the need for genuine references, as integrity is a crucial aspect of this process.

A helpful tip is to include "Excellent References Available on Request" if you've received positive feedback from your referees. The word "excellent" carries significant weight and can enhance your candidacy. If asked about the excellence of your references during an interview, you can highlight your strengths, such as outstanding customer service, receiving awards, taking on additional responsibilities, maintaining a positive attitude, and consistently meeting deadlines.

If they don't have any, they can write this statement on their CV: "References available on request."

Don't Upload Your CV on Job Sites

This is another word of advice you should pass on to your child. Uploading their CV on job boards can pose challenges and may hinder their application in multiple ways.

Initially, these platforms attract a diverse pool of job seekers with varying qualifications and experiences, potentially causing their CV to be lost among numerous applications, thereby diminishing its visibility to potential employers.

Additionally, when they upload their CV to a job board, it becomes accessible to a wide audience, including their current employer or colleagues. This accessibility may jeopardise their current position or professional relationships, leading to potential conflicts or complications.

Tailoring their CV to align with a specific job advertisement is crucial. This tailored approach showcases their understanding of the employer's requirements and highlights their relevant skills and experiences. Uploading a generic CV to job boards fails to convey this tailored approach, thereby reducing its appeal to employers and decreasing the likelihood of standing out amidst competing candidates.

Additionally, neglecting to customise their CV using keywords for the targeted job opportunity means missing the chance to emphasise specific experiences, skills, and achievements that directly match the role's requirements. Consequently, this oversight diminishes the prospects of their application being noticed by recruiters or hiring managers seeking candidates with precisely aligned qualifications and attributes.

The only time that this is effective is if you're a student or graduate seeking seasonal work or travel funds. If so, consider uploading your CV to Indeed. For more established professionals, adding the green "open to work" banner can attract direct contact from recruiters. I am not an advocate of uploading your CV to job sites, but it's worth noting that many agencies, especially those hiring for frontline roles in hospitality or seasonal positions, actively search Indeed for candidates. A standout CV can make a positive impression in these searches, so there may not be a significant downside to uploading it.

Review the first parts of this chapter as it goes into more detail about crafting an effective CV for the desired role rather than a blanket approach.

Common Mistakes to Avoid

In the pursuit of creating an effective and compelling CV, it's crucial to steer clear of common pitfalls. Young applicants often fall victim to these errors, which can hinder their chances in a competitive job market.

Failure to tailor the CV to the specific job application

I must emphasise: The job advert is already giving your child the answers to the question, "What should I put in my CV?" So they must write their CV accordingly, i.e.

if it is looking for exceptional customer service skills, then guess what? Your child has exactly these skills.

Poor formatting

Overly complex designs or templates often distract rather than impress. Of course, if your child is going for a design, creative, modelling or even a beauty role, where design and image are important, then they may add a photo and funky design. If not, they can stick to two pages, a straightforward font like Arial, and should use bullet points, not essays.

Short, sharp and clear

As mentioned above, CVs should ideally be no more than two pages and the font no smaller than 11. Anything longer may not get read, whereas a font that is smaller (or a creative font) makes it hard to read.

Omitting key information

These include neglecting to write essential details about education and experience, as these leave gaps in your abilities and experiences, which ultimately leads to missed opportunities. It is worth detailing what training courses your child has been on. Are they a first aider? Have they done any customer service training? Computing certificates? Encourage your child to really think about and go through all their certificates and honours.

Tell your child not to put their CV on the job board
Unless they are going for a temporary or seasonal role. If not every CV needs to be tailored to the role, with keywords and great examples of why they would suit the job. As detailed in point 1.

Once they have written their CV it's time to tailor their cover letter. The letter should be enthusiastic and showcase the research they have done on that company, stating the reason they would like to apply for the role. This is similar to the personal statement but it clearly states "I am writing to apply for the role of [role] advertised on / in [where]...."

Characteristics of a good cover letters include:

Being tailored to the organisation and job role they are applying for
They can highlight their most relevant skills and experience, demonstrating that they have researched the company and the job. They should write a cover letter for each application, and research the company to customise it effectively. What are the company's

missions and values and how does the candidate align with them?

Having a good strong opening statement

Candidates should clearly express why they want the job and what they bring to the table. "I am applying for the role of [Job role] advertised on [where the advert is] as I am a graduate of ... having studied for ... or I have ... [years, relevant] experience or ... having previously worked as... [relevance for role]"

Being brief whilst emphasising the candidate's suitability for the job

It should be no more than one page, ideally five to six paragraphs maximum. If a recruiter normally takes seven seconds to read a CV, then the cover letter should make them want to spend more time reading about the candidate.

Personalised to a specific addressee as much as possible

They must address the cover letter to a specific person whenever possible, especially if the hiring Manager is known. If not, "To whom it may concern:" should suffice. It should look professional, use the right language and tone, and be double-checked for spelling and grammar. Approximately 59% of recruiters will reject a candidate because of poor grammar or a spelling error, as these mistakes indicate that the candidate is sloppy and hasn't taken the time to proofread their CV. Additionally, 43% of CVs are discarded due to spelling or grammatical mistakes, making it very likely that a CV will be rejected if such errors are present. Therefore, it is crucial to ensure that your child's CV is free from spelling and grammatical mistakes to avoid being rejected.

Many entry-level positions are posted on Indeed, resulting in a large pool of applicants

However, many candidates overlook the importance of including a cover letter. Adding a tailored cover letter that addresses the job requirements can significantly boost your application's visibility. A well-crafted cover letter showcasing your skills and experience relevant to the role can greatly enhance your chances of being contacted by employers.

Exercise 4

To summarise this chapter, here is a checklist that will help your child ensure they have an effective CV that is ultimately aimed at getting an interview.

Personal Information
- Full name, town, and county and postcode
- Contact details and a professionally oriented email address
- Correct mobile/contact number

Personal Statement
- Briefly introduce the candidate, their key strengths, interest in the role they are applying for, and their desire to work for the company they are applying to
- Use this portion as an opportunity to get some key words in

Key Skills
- Showcase a diverse range of competencies
- Emphasise skills such as time management, communication, adaptability, problem-solving, teamwork, creativity, leadership, interpersonal skills, work ethic, attention to detail

Professional Achievements/Certifications

- Showcase noteworthy accomplishments
- Highlight academic or extracurricular achievements

Education

- Include details of academic qualifications and ongoing studies
- List each subject and grades, especially if the candidate scored high

Work Experience/Work History

- Highlight relevant work experience, including part-time jobs, internships, or volunteer work
- Detail what they did in each role using bullet points

Hobbies

- Include some hobbies or interests
- Avoid overly whacky hobbies
- Write 2 or 3 lines and provide details rather than just list sport, travel, music

References

- Get a recommendation and references if leaving school, college, or university

Finally, encourage your child to practise looking at job adverts and highlight the key words they are asking for, just like a specification list for a new phone, car or house. What do the hirers need that they, as candidates, can fulfil?

If they used AI for creating both the CV and cover letter, it should be 80% fit for the purpose. AI is only as good as the prompts you put in, so you must personalise and refine whatever output AI creates.

Unless you are an exceptional prompt navigator or creator, AI still needs the human element. It *will* make you more efficient with these steps. And although it normally uses American spelling if you don't prompt it to write in British English, use of AI should help with spelling, punctuation and grammar.

Your child should now be armed and ready to apply for a job!

"Networking is not about just connecting people. It's about connecting people with people, people with ideas, and people with opportunities."

– Michele Jennae

Chapter 5
Step 4: The Power of Networking

"Opportunities do not float like clouds in the sky. They're attached to people. If you're looking for an opportunity, you're really looking for a person."

– Ben Casnocha

One of the most powerful tools you can help your child develop is a strong network. In today's competitive job market, the significance of networking cannot be underestimated.

Welcome to step 4 in the strategy, where we focus on empowering you to support your child's career journey through the strategic use of networking. As parents, your role in nurturing and guiding your children towards success is so important. Networking is a competitive edge tool that parents don't use enough and they should.

Networking has evolved into more than just a professional practice; it's a fundamental skill that can open doors and create opportunities for your child's future. In this chapter, we'll explore how you can effectively leverage networking to help your child navigate the job market more quickly and efficiently.

Throughout this chapter, I will show the numerous benefits of networking, from expanding your child's circle of contacts to providing them with valuable insights and potential job leads. By understanding the power of networking, you can empower your child to build meaningful connections that can shape their career now and in the future.

Finally, I'll outline a couple of things you can do with your child to prepare them for success in the professional world. By focusing on optimising their online presence, participating in networking events, and understanding the importance of networking, you can help set your child on the path to a successful career.

Lastly, if this fills you with dread and you, yourself don't network or aren't confident enough in that department, I guarantee you know someone who does. Who in your friends and family have a LinkedIn profile or account? Who goes to a networking group, or is confident at asking for help? You do have a network, you just don't know you have one yet.

What Is Networking?

Networking involves establishing and nurturing mutually beneficial relationships. It's about connecting with people who can offer guidance, support, and opportunities for career or business growth. These connections can be made through various channels, including friends, family, colleagues, social media, professional events, and industry-specific gatherings. *This is your network.*

The Benefits of Networking

I believe a lot of things in life come from the saying "It's not what you know but who you know."

Sometimes we don't know what we need but we may know someone who can help. Don't underestimate how big your network is and how you can help your child. If you have a Facebook or LinkedIn account, just count how many followers you have, how many people you work with or talk to, and how many friends and family are on there as well?

This also doesn't have to be all on social media. Are you part of a local choir group or sports club? Think about the school and the parents or teachers that go to the school. Your network and networking aren't all about standing up for one minute in a room of people at 6:00 am in the morning.

It is what I call your Opportunity: Who among the people you know are available to lend support?

Here are some statistics to show the power of a network.

70% of jobs are not advertised: This statistic is often attributed to the "hidden job market," where many job opportunities are filled through informal channels such as networking, referrals, and direct communication with employers.

85% of vacancies are filled via referrals: A significant portion of job placements occurs through recommendations from existing employees. Similar to the first statistic, the specific source may vary, but it's commonly used to highlight the impact of networking on job opportunities.

It's essential to understand that even as students, your children possess a significant network that extends beyond what might be immediately apparent. Reflecting on my experience conducting a workshop at a local college, I discovered a prevailing misconception among students.

Many felt that networking was only relevant when engaging with professional businesses or larger corporations to secure work experience. This revelation highlighted a missed opportunity within their immediate academic, lifestyle and wider community and connections.

As parents, it's crucial to help your children recognise the diverse potential for networking, not only within established industries but also within the supportive environment of friends and family. Encouraging them to appreciate the significance of building relationships early on is key, emphasising that networking goes beyond conventional corporate settings, and can be a powerful tool for their personal and professional development.

Here are a few questions I ask students when I run sessions on networking, as it opens up a lot of ideas for them to try:

1. Who do you know in your family that works in a business (any size business)? Make a list.
2. Who among your connections could help connect you to other people that could provide support? Think friends, family, social clubs, sports clubs, churches or communities you are part of.
3. Do any of your family and friends go to business networking groups or are they on LinkedIn
4. Which 3 people would you approach that you think could help?

Building and Expanding Your Network

Encourage your child to build business connections by attending career fairs organised by schools, colleges, and universities. These events provide a chance for them to meet potential employers in a more informal setting, away from the formalities of an interview. Share the impact of personal connections by highlighting instances where individuals hired at recruitment fairs wouldn't have applied if they hadn't made that initial connection.

Consider accompanying your child to a trade fair or advising them to seek assistance from their careers team. Suggest that they bring along copies of their CV and actively engage in conversations to gain hands-on experience while exploring potential companies. Encourage your child to reach out to tutors, lecturers, or the careers team for valuable support.

These mentors can offer insights and may have connections in the industry or role your child is interested in. Promote the idea of networking on LinkedIn, urging them to connect with mentors and explore relevant groups to broaden their understanding of the industry. This proactive approach creates valuable connections and industry knowledge for your child's professional journey.

Encourage your child to take a proactive approach by personally visiting shops, entertainment venues, or offices to inquire about job opportunities. Advise them to ask for the best person to speak to and either hand their CV directly to them or obtain their email address. When emailing their CV, suggest they personalise it with a brief covering letter mentioning their recent visit and interaction. For instance, they could say, "During my visit to the store today, I spoke with Heather, who kindly provided me with your email address.

I am excited about the opportunity to..." This proactive approach can greatly enhance their chances of securing employment.

Guide your child in setting up a LinkedIn profile to stay updated on industry news, follow companies of interest, and access information on new developments and jobs in their chosen industry. This proactive approach ensures that your child remains informed and ahead of the competition. If they are already on social media it should be easy for them to do, as it's the same as liking and following people on other platforms like Instagram or TikTok.

How Parents Can Help?

When thinking about your network and what opportunities that it could offer your child, it's important to highlight that networks extend beyond professional contacts. Your network encompasses a diverse array of individuals, from friends and family members to acquaintances and colleagues.

It's not just about the quantity of people you know, but also about the quality of relationships and the different perspectives they offer. Recognising the value of your connections can greatly benefit your child as they navigate their career paths.

By leveraging your network, whether it's seeking advice, exploring job opportunities, or gaining insights into various industries, you can help tap into valuable resources to support your child's career growth. As parents or guardians, understanding the breadth and depth of your network can provide valuable guidance and support to your children as they pursue their professional aspirations.

Here's an example.

I did a one-minute introduction to my business at a networking event and was talking about helping T level students with work placements, following a session I had run at the local college. I was looking for accountants to help and I wanted to help the college place 11 students.

I also talked about how their parents could help. A member of my networking group said "My son is studying and needs a work placement." I didn't even think to ask, but he then realised we had a room full of people who could help his son and his class. As we are a networking group, we are now working to look into our own networks to place all his friends too!

Help introduce your child to people who may be able to help, provide advice, and open doors if you have personal connections. However, please let your child implement the search, apply and handle the follow-up, and establish their own employer-employee relationships. It's important for your child to be seen as a future employee, and not your child.

Here are some practical steps parents can take to help their child get hired using their network:

Introduce your child to your network

This includes introducing them to not just your professional network, but also your friends, colleagues, and acquaintances who might be able to provide job opportunities or advice. But it's important that the child takes the initiative to follow up and build these relationships. Take them to your network group as a guest if you are a member of one.

Teach networking skills

You can teach your child how to network effectively, with tasks like approaching people properly, starting conversations, making meaningful handshakes, asking insightful questions, and following up after meetings.

Encourage independence

While you can provide support and guidance, it's important for the child to take the lead in their job search. Taking over and being too involved will diminish your child's credibility, and the job will become more about you than them finishing and securing it themselves.

Promote balance

Encourage your child to balance their job search with other responsibilities and activities. Set two mornings a week when your child focuses on job searching and application management. Set 20 mins a day from Monday to Friday for increasing their network and doing industry research, reading insight, liking and documenting relevant LinkedIn posts. Then allow them to do other things. When people say job searching is a full-time job, don't believe them. It's not and should never be! Teach your child to set boundaries and focus.

Model good networking behaviour

Explain to your child the importance of good networking behaviour, such as looking smart, being respectful, listening actively, and showing genuine interest in other people's business.

Help them prepare

Review their CV, and prepare them for professional communication, like practising interview questions. When I mentor students, they tend to waffle and over think the answers, so help them be more focused in their answers

Remember, the goal is not to do the work for your child, but to guide and support them. I meet so many students that don't get support from their tutors or their parents, mainly because they don't know what to ask for. They don't know how to write a CV and don't get the support. The lecturer and work coaches don't have time to do it for them. Any support you can give to your child will help them massively. You don't have to be an expert, you just need to see what opportunity you have in your network that can support your child who could help with a CV or job opportunity.

By understanding the importance of networking, creating strong LinkedIn profiles, and actively engaging in networking events or online communities, your child can maximise their opportunities to get hired and advance their careers.

Don't overthink it, I bet you will know someone who can help or at least introduce them to someone who does, even if it's for some advice.

Lastly, supporting your child in their career journey involves avoiding the assumption that the strategies or paths that worked for you will necessarily yield the same results for them. Each individual's career path is unique, and the current professional landscape is significantly different from what it once was.

Exercise 5

To finish this Chapter, pick one of the three things to do to actively help your child expand their network and increase their opportunity to get hired and build a successful career.

1. **Help set up or review their LinkedIn profile:**
    This includes ensuring it is complete and up-to-date, using a professional-looking photo, crafting a compelling summary, and highlighting their achievements. Encourage them to actively engage with connections and relevant content on the platform.

2. **Encourage networking participation:**
    Support your child in joining networking events, career fairs, and industry-specific gatherings. Additionally, encourage their involvement in online communities such as industry-specific forums, webinars and LinkedIn groups.

3. **Facilitate real-world networking opportunities:**

   If appropriate, consider bringing your child into your workplace or taking them to professional networking events. This can provide them with firsthand experience of professional environments and the opportunity to observe and learn networking skills in action.

"Many of life's failures are people who did not realize how close they were to success when they gave up." – Thomas Edison

Chapter 6
Step 5: Job Application Management and Support

"All our dreams can come true—if we have the courage to pursue them." – Walt Disney

Sending that first CV and application can be a daunting experience, especially when it involves your child. In this chapter, you will learn how to provide guidance on critical elements that can significantly impact the success of your child's job application.

Staying positive whilst supporting and helping your child through the challenges with resilience and determination is key. If they get the email to say their application has not been successful, this may be their first experience of being rejected. It can be disheartening and may affect their confidence if not rationalised. We'll explore the importance of a timely application, crafting a focused CV, and recapping some points already covered in Chapter 4.

The Early Bird Catches the Worm

Prime Talent (individuals ideally suited for a specific role, whether it be due to their experience, energy, behaviours, or demonstration of the desired traits for the position) are often hired within 10 days.

It's crucial to note that many job adverts mention the possibility of closing the application process early. Waiting until the last application date may result in missed opportunities. Therefore, it is highly recommended to apply promptly, ensuring your candidacy is considered in the initial stages of the selection process.

When looking for a job it shouldn't take over your life. Although easy to say, it can very quickly take over your child's, and they can quickly become overwhelmed, desperate or withdrawn, as it can appear to be such a hard and unenjoyable thing to do.

I suggest job hunting twice a week. When doing this, select only those jobs that have been posted within seven days. Don't forget you are searching for keywords and not job titles.

Get your child to apply for three to five jobs at a time. They should make a log of who they have applied to so that they don't lose track of their job applications. Some adverts say if you haven't heard back within two weeks you have been unsuccessful. Log that, and if your child hasn't heard from them, they can move on. It's just not meant to be, so tell them not to sweat over it.

As a Japanese proverb wisely says, "Fall seven times, stand up eight."

I have coached and mentored clients who have sent three CVs, got two interviews, and have been hired. For some people applying in competitive job markets, it may take up to 20 applications. But keep going and don't give up.

I've been reviewing insights on LinkedIn statistics regarding job applications. It appears to show that 200 individuals have applied for an advertised role, when in practice this is not the case, because LinkedIn also tracks other metrics such as views and opens. It's important not to be discouraged by these figures.

Additionally, the results reveal information about applicants with a degree or those who are only a 70% match for the job. This shouldn't dissuade your child. It simply indicates that their profile may lack certain keywords necessary to align with the required skills, which they may not have the option of including.

Dealing with Rejection

When children experience rejection in their job search, they are likely to feel a range of emotions, including disappointment, frustration, and a blow to their confidence. As parents, it's important to provide support and guidance during this time. Encourage them to acknowledge their feelings, emphasising the competitive nature of the job market, and highlighting their strengths to help boost their confidence.

Consider relaying the analogy of embarking on a committed relationship as a metaphor for navigating career choices. Reflect on the number of dates one might go on before finding the right match. Similarly, in the realm of careers, individuals may need to explore various professional experiences before discovering their ideal fit.

Just as not everyone falls in love at first sight or marries their childhood sweetheart, the same can be said about finding the perfect job match. As a career coach, I encourage clients to recognise that the journey toward a fulfilling career may involve facing challenges and undergoing growth before discovering a role that brings true professional satisfaction.

The analogy serves as a reminder that, like the dating process, exploring diverse career opportunities is essential before committing to a long-term professional path.

Preparing Your Child for a Changing Career Landscape

As a parent, it's natural to want to provide your child with a clear, straightforward path to career success. However, the reality of the modern workforce is quite different from the traditional model of a single, lifelong career. Recent data suggests that individuals may have an average of 12 to 15 distinct careers over the course of their working lives.

This shift reflects the increasingly dynamic and evolving nature of work. Factors like technological advancements, changing skill demands, and a greater emphasis on work-life balance have led many workers to re-evaluate their career trajectories and make significant transitions. Job tenure and organisational loyalty have declined, with employees changing roles and companies more frequently, especially among younger generations.

As you guide your child through their educational and career journey, it's important to help them develop the mindset and skills needed to navigate this shifting landscape. Encourage them to grow and develop a versatile skill set, maintain career agility, and be open to new opportunities. Emphasise the value of continuous learning, adaptability, and the ability to transfer skills across different roles and industries.

By preparing your child for the reality of multiple career changes, you can empower them to embrace the evolving nature of work and position themselves for long-term success. With the right guidance and support, they can thrive in this dynamic environment and find fulfilment in their professional lives.

Rejection Due to a Poor CV or Social Media Profile

In today's digital age, prospective companies often review social media profiles as part of their candidate evaluation process. As such, you must let your child know the potential impact their online personas can have on job applications.

The following statistics serve as a guide to help both you and your child understand why they may be rejected solely based on social media evaluations. These numbers shed light on the factors that contribute to rejection. Recognising these aspects is essential for ensuring that your profile represents you in the best possible light within the competitive job market.

- 75% don't like seeing offensive language on social media so they will reject the application
- 70% get concerned about any mentions of drug use
- 50% worry if there are mistakes in spelling and grammar in their posts
- 47% reject due to drunken behaviour or pictures
- 29% reject on political views

So, it's a good idea for your child to regularly check and review their social media profiles to make sure they look professional and won't cause any issues when applying for jobs.

As stated above 50% of businesses reject the application looking at the grammar of social media posts and 77% reject applications based on grammatical errors on their CV. I work with colleges, schools, universities and job centres. On one occasion I was working with a college student who signed a cover letter without using capital letters in their own name. Although it seems obvious to us, the next generation don't value grammar like we do. Please take the time to review your child's CV and cover letters.

Some children are over-using AI, and you can tell their entire CV and cover letter is crafted by AI. For example, AI-created content uses American spelling (using z instead of s), and AI-generated cover letters are written this way.

I was talking about this with my husband, and he said they rejected a CV for this very thing. The candidate had a lot of experience and may have been a good fit for the job. But the position he was applying for was writing project briefs, and using British English grammar and spelling was so central to this specific role. It was so important they rejected the candidate without even speaking to him.

If I had £1 for every business owner who has told me, "Heather, when you assist these individuals, please emphasise the importance of having no typos in their CVs", I would definitely be so many pounds richer. They often express frustration, noting that they've rejected 80% of CVs solely due to spelling errors. It's crucial to take the time to ensure grammatical accuracy in your CV.

Some HR professionals are avid social media sleuths; upon receiving a job application, they may scour social media accounts for additional insights. So please advise your child to review and remove potentially harmful content that could affect their career prospects.

Try to ensure and check your child's social media profiles as well, or at least ask them the question: If I was an employer looking at your profile, would I hire you?

Your Child's Online Presence

As discussed in Chapter 5, networking is a key strategy in securing employment. And although an online presence isn't essential, having a professional profile can help assist your child getting hired.

Statistics show that having an online presence is crucial for job seekers, as approximately 84% of UK employers utilise social media for recruitment—with 96% relying on LinkedIn and 66% on Facebook, along with other social media platforms.

Recruitment often parallels sales and marketing strategies, utilising platforms tailored to attract candidates effectively. LinkedIn is a prime hub for professionals aged 24 to 45, while Facebook caters more to individuals aged 35 to 60.

Younger generations gravitate towards platforms like TikTok and X, which have yet to be widely embraced in recruitment circles. Establishing a LinkedIn account is important for your child's career prospects, as it offers the opportunity to be approached for jobs without having to look.

In today's digital-first world, recruiters and hiring managers are increasingly turning to LinkedIn to identify and connect with prime talent. In fact, the global recruiter population on LinkedIn has grown significantly in recent years, with nearly 1 million talent acquisition professionals now active on the platform. This means that having a well-crafted, optimised LinkedIn profile can significantly boost your child's visibility and open the door to valuable career opportunities. By highlighting their skills, experience, and personal brand, your child can position themselves as an attractive candidate that recruiters are actively seeking out.

LinkedIn provides tools that allow users to connect with industry peers, join relevant communities, and stay up-to-date on the latest trends—all of which can give your child a competitive edge in their job search. Encouraging your child to invest time and effort into building a strong LinkedIn presence is an impactful way to help them stand out and get discovered by the right people at the right time.

They can also utilise the "open to work" feature to signal to recruiters their interest in opportunities within the specific job titles they've highlighted. This is particularly beneficial if they have an established career track record.

The Power of Recruitment Agencies

If the jobs your child is interested in are being posted by recruiters, apply directly to some of the recruitment agencies in their target industry. These agencies have established relationships with companies and can actively search for relevant opportunities on your child's behalf. Working with a great recruitment agent can be a game-changer, providing access to roles that may not be publicly advertised.

I was fortunate enough to partner with a recruitment agent for 14 years, and he placed me in four different positions during that time. His industry reputation and connections helped me secure interviews I may not have otherwise received. A skilled recruiter can truly become a valuable long-term ally, advocating for your child and opening doors to exciting new opportunities.

My recruiter not only found me great roles, but he also became a trusted friend. Even 20 years later, we still work together—a testament to the power of building a strong, collaborative relationship. The insights, guidance, and personalised support a good recruiter provides are worth their weight in gold. By registering with reputable agencies in your child's field, you can give them a significant advantage in their job search and career development.

Rather than letting them rely solely on job boards and online applications, encourage your child to research and connect with local recruitment firms. These partners can provide CV feedback, interview preparation, and insider knowledge to help your child stand out. With their support and access to exclusive opportunities, your child will be well-positioned to launch a rewarding career.

Encourage your child to sign up with an agency that specialises in roles matching their interests. High street agencies are great for local admin, industrial, or driving jobs. For hospitality roles at sporting events, music festivals, bars, and restaurants, there are numerous agencies to explore. Let them do research to identify agencies that are likely to assist them. Remember, agencies typically work with candidates they believe they can place successfully. Before contacting them, suggest that your child checks their website to see if they specialise in the types of roles they're seeking.

Here are some top tips that will help your child stand out to recruitment agencies:

Encourage them to prepare their CV
Make sure that your child updates their CV, and that it highlights their skills, experiences, and unique selling points. Recruitment consultants will use this to match them with relevant opportunities, so make it as strong as possible.

Communicate their goals
Your child has to be clear and upfront with the recruitment agency about the type of role, industry, salary, and location they are targeting. This will help agencies identify the best-fit opportunities for your child.

Leverage the agency's expertise

Take advantage of the recruitment consultant's industry knowledge and connections. Your child should ask for advice on tailoring their CV, preparing for interviews, and navigating the job market.

Maintain open communication

Your child should be staying in regular contact with their recruitment consultant, updating them on their job search progress and any changes in their preferences or circumstances. This will keep them top-of-mind for new opportunities.

Tell them to be open to temporary/contract roles or suggested roles the recruiters believe they could do

It's important for your child to listen to their recruiter. If they have built a good relationship and they understand your child's skills, agents may introduce your child to a role or company they think your child would excel in. Be open and trust their experience.

Be loyal!

Don't let your child sign up to hundreds of agencies. There is nothing worse for a recruiter or recruitment partner to see that a candidate is with a number of recruitment agents, or that employers get the same CV from three different companies. Although on the outset it looks like they are keen, it also comes across as slightly desperate and having a lack of commitment.

As a recruiter we have to send additional emails with proof to show who we received the CV from first. In my experience, that leaves a bad taste as the recruiter will have asked if they have applied to other agencies, and it means that the candidate has sometimes not been truthful.

If your child is doing research on recruiters, tell them to look for industry standards like Ofsted for apprenticeship providers. The inspections are as hard as school inspections, so when you have companies rated as outstanding, they really value and look after their apprenticeships. I work with some partners just like my recruitment agent and they really care about the individuals. You will notice that some providers are just churning numbers; it will appear that they are only looking at placing job-seekers, rather than finding a company fit for the job-seeker for long-term retention.

Look for testimonials, referrals and recommendations, a bit like you would if you were travelling. Look through Glassdoor, Trustpilot, the agency's websites, other students or candidates. Also check how long ago the testimonials were written.

Agencies highly value strong recommendations. If a friend has had success with an agency, they're more inclined to meet with your child. Even better, if a family member or relative is a client, the recruitment consultant may go the extra mile to assist your child or provide advice.

The Dangers of Relying on Benefits After Graduation

While government benefits may provide a temporary safety net, encourage your child to avoid them as much as possible when leaving college or university. In my opinion this is a great life lesson for their long-term success.

I have worked with many young people who have become complacent living on universal credit or jobseeker's allowance, as it reduces the urgency and motivation to actively pursue meaningful employment or other goals. This can lead to a cycle of dependency and a diminished sense of purpose.

If there is a financial urgency in order to live (such as stated in Chapter 1) by all means apply. But I have found it can be a hindrance for young people.

Encourage your child instead to think about the lifestyle they want, whether it's driving a certain car, upgrading their phone, or saving up for travel. By shifting the conversation to these tangible, motivating goals, you can inspire them to take proactive steps to earn the money needed to achieve those dreams.

While the safety net of benefits may be necessary in some cases, your role as a parent should be to challenge your child to aim higher and take ownership of their financial future.

Managing Your Child's Application Recap

As mentioned previously, I recommend establishing a structured job-hunting routine for your child, suggesting a twice-weekly session.

Focus on selecting and applying to jobs posted within the last seven days, emphasising the use of keywords rather than job titles during the search. Encourage your child to apply for three to five jobs simultaneously through job boards, maintaining a log of applications to prevent overwhelm and track progress.

Some job postings specify a response timeframe, usually within two to four weeks, so note these on the log. If there's no response, advise them to move on and not dwell on it; not every opportunity is meant to be.

I recommend checking job boards, company websites, and industry newsletters on social media twice a week to stay abreast of the latest job postings. This structured approach ensures consistency and helps manage the job-hunting process effectively.

To enhance your child's job-hunting strategy, encourage them to sign up with a reputable recruitment partner or agency. Conduct thorough research, reading reviews, and seeking recommendations from your network to ensure a reliable choice. Emphasise the importance of applying promptly to job postings, maintaining professionalism on social media profiles, and meticulously reviewing applications for typos or grammatical errors. Aligning the CV and cover letter with keywords from the job advertisement is crucial for a strong application.

Supporting your child's resilience throughout the process is essential. In case they haven't found a suitable position, redirect their focus to apprenticeships, temporary contracts, or volunteering opportunities. This not only provides valuable experience but also boosts confidence and expands their skill set. Encourage them to learn from any feedback received, utilising it constructively to enhance application and interview skills. Recognise that continuous improvement is integral to being a resilient job seeker.

Setting realistic expectations is key. Remind your child that rejection is a natural part of the job-hunting process. Encourage them to maintain perseverance, understanding that the right opportunity may take time to materialise. Emphasise that resilience, continuous learning, and realistic expectations form the foundation for a successful and enduring job search. Don't let them take it personally, just keep following the process.

There are hundreds of free or affordable training courses that can be completed online. If your child hasn't got much experience, completing these will show commitments and learning ability. It is also a very productive use of time for your child whilst applying.

Celebrate Small Wins
Acknowledge and celebrate every step forward, whether it's securing an interview or receiving positive feedback. This positive reinforcement fuels resilience and maintains their motivation. Celebrate the interviews like it's the best thing that's ever happened! If your child secures interviews, they are one step closer to securing a job.

Don't focus on the job itself as the ultimate goal. Instead, shift the emphasis to celebrating the incremental progress and achievements along the way. Each successful interview, positive interaction with a recruiter, or constructive feedback should be recognised and applauded. This approach serves two key purposes:

1. It reinforces the value of their efforts and hard work, keeping them encouraged and motivated to continue pushing forward.

2. It helps shift the mindset away from solely fixating on the end result (the job), and instead appreciating the journey and learning opportunities that come with each step.

By consistently celebrating the small wins, you're providing your child with the positive reinforcement and resilience they need to navigate the ups and downs of the job search process. This fuels their determination and prevents discouragement, ultimately increasing the chances of them securing their desired role. Remember, the path to success is rarely straightforward.

Embracing and commemorating each milestone, no matter how small, can make all the difference in maintaining your child's momentum and confidence.

Exercise 6

Review your child's CV, cover letter, or profile for spelling mistakes, professionalism and accuracy.

This will most likely be the most important thing you do to help secure your child a job!

"Anything is possible once you believe you are worthy of achieving it."

– Jason Pockrandt

Chapter 7
Step 6: A Competitive Edge Interview Strategy

"One important key to success is self-confidence. An important key to self-confidence is preparation."
– Arthur Ashe

As a parent, one of the most valuable gifts you can give your child is the gift of self-confidence. This powerful trait not only shapes their overall outlook on life, but it can also be a make-or-break factor when it comes to succeeding in job interviews.

When your child steps into an interview setting, their level of self-confidence can have a profound impact on their performance. Candidates who exude self-assurance (not arrogance, see Chapter 4) tend to come across as more poised, articulate, and capable—

qualities that can give them a distinct competitive edge. They are better able to effectively communicate their skills, highlight their unique value, and project an aura of competence that resonates with interviewers.

On the flip side, a lack of self-confidence can be a significant hindrance. Children who struggle with self-doubt may appear nervous, hesitant, or even defensive during an interview. They may have difficulty making eye contact, speaking up, or conveying their strengths with conviction. This can lead to a missed opportunity, as interviewers may interpret these behaviours as a lack of enthusiasm, preparation, or suitability for the role.

As a parent, you have the power to shape your child's self-confidence and equip them with the tools to shine in any interview setting. Develop an environment of encouragement, praise, and positive reinforcement from an early age. Celebrate their successes, no matter how small, and help them develop a growth mindset that embraces challenges as opportunities for learning and improvement.

Encourage your child to step outside their comfort zone and take on new experiences that build a sense of accomplishments and growth. Whether it's being confident in social situations, participating in extracurricular activities, or taking on leadership roles, these experiences can boost their confidence and prepare them to handle the high-pressure situation of a job interview.

Most importantly, model self-confidence yourself. When your child sees you navigating life's ups and downs with calm and self-assurance, they're more likely to do the same. Share the ways you deal with nerves or staying positive—that gives them a roadmap to follow.

For example, if you have tricks for calming down before a big meeting, tell your child about them. Or explain how you remind yourself of your strengths when you're feeling unsure. Showing them the strategies, you use can help them develop their own confidence.

The key is being open about how you manage challenging situations. That way, your child has real-life examples to learn from. They can see how you project confidence, even when you might be feeling nervous inside.

By nurturing your child's self-confidence from an early age, you're not only setting them up for success in the interview room, but you're also equipping them with a valuable life skill that will serve them well in all their future endeavours. With a strong sense of self-belief, your child will be poised to make a lasting impression and secure the opportunities they deserve.

Recruitment Costs

It's apparent that our children often lack an understanding of the effort and cost involved in the recruitment and retention process.

This isn't due to any fault of their own; rather, they simply haven't had the experience of buying, working, and investing in the same way we have. Therefore, it's crucial to engage them in conversations about the intricacies of these processes, helping them grasp the significance of their actions and decisions.

Drawing from my own experience conducting sales training in retail and IT help desks, I frequently highlighted the substantial costs spent by customers for products and services. Whether it was a kitchen, bathroom, or bedroom ranging from £3,000 to £30,000, understanding these expenses was paramount for effective sales and service. Remarkably, many of the individuals I trained, typically aged between 16 and 22, had only ever purchased relatively inexpensive items like mobile phones or second-hand cars. Their limited exposure to significant financial transactions underscored their unfamiliarity with the true value of money, time and commitment. Explaining the sacrifices and how long customers took to make buying decisions gave them greater respect for the sales process and service.

This also needs to be considered with the financial investment required by companies in the recruitment process, averaging around £3,000 per position just to advertise. On top of this figure there are additional expenses such as management time, onboarding, training, equipment, and uniform. Furthermore, there are significant percentages (11-20%) of initial salary paid to recruitment agencies.

With this financial commitment it is important to educate your child to take the process seriously, to prepare properly and to show up on time for the interview.

A 1-in-3 Chance for Your Child
There is a misconception that employers interview loads of people, in fact it's usually only 3 candidates who get through to a face to face interview. In my two decades of experience that applicants effectively face a

1-in-3 chance of securing the position once they have been granted an interview.

I'll say it again: Your child gets a 1-in-3 chance to get hired.

I often hear parents talk about how their child got an opportunity for an interview and pulled out. It makes me want to confront them not only as a huge missed opportunity for them but also a waste of valuable time for the business.

LinkedIn mentions that "a striking 93% of 18- to 24-year-olds in the UK admitted to missing scheduled job interviews". Please don't let your child be one of these statistics.

This is the final step of the Six-Step Strategy, and we will cover the why and the how of it, as well as what the consequences are if your child doesn't prepare. In this chapter, I will equip you with the insights and strategies needed to help your child navigate the job market with confidence and poise.

With your unwavering support and the tools outlined here, your child will be empowered to showcase their unique strengths, communicate their value, and ultimately secure the opportunities they deserve.

First Impressions Count

It takes less than three seconds for someone to make a first impression, whether it is good or bad.

In the context of an interview, when you are greeted in reception, how you have walked in to say you have an interview—these are all first impressions. Right or wrong, it's human nature for people to make judgements based on what you wear, how you look, and what you say.

It takes, on average, 1,000 words to undo a bad first impression, so here is how to make the best first impression your child can provide.

How to Prepare for an Interview

In the UK, a staggering 84% of employers believe that a lack of preparation in candidates is a significant barrier to a successful interview.

99.99% of interviews will ask "Tell me what you know about the company and role." Why? They want to know you have done some research and actually want a job. Some employers are put off and have had bad experiences as they interview people that don't either really want the job, are just doing the interview to tick a box to gain government benefits, or "My mum or dad said I need to do it."

Here are just a few sample questions to research and prepare for. Type these into an internet search engine or AI:

- When was the company founded?
- What does the company do?
- Who are their clients and customers?
- What is their vision, values and mission?
- What do they sell?
- How many offices do they have? Are they global?

Why do they ask this? When I was working in IT and interviewing prospects, I came across some awful answers, such as, "Dunno... you just do IT..." and then silence. In the IT company, we had different sectors: We did software, tech and web solutions. So many other answers were available, but the one answer I got from the candidates were terribly inadequate. We spent thousands on recruitment, and the individuals couldn't be bothered to research the company.

I can't stress enough the importance of being prepared as a minimum with the questions above. This not only demonstrates genuine interest, but also equips your child to tailor their response to align with the company they are interviewing with.

Every interview will have some form of competency-based questions, so coach them on articulating their responses with confidence. HR and line managers will routinely ask the same questions to all candidates. This is usually:

1. What do you know about the business and role?
2. Tell me about yourself and why you would be a good fit for the role?
3. Customer-based question: In an interview, a customer-based question is designed to gauge the candidate's proficiency in comprehending and addressing customer needs effectively. *An example of this would be, can you share a specific experience where you successfully addressed a customer's concern or issue? Tell me how you identified the problem, communicated with the customer and resolved the issue.*
4. Problem-based question: On the other hand, a problem-based question aims to assess the candidate's problem-solving skills and their

approach to overcoming challenges in a professional setting. *An example of this would be, give me an example of a problem you have experienced in your previous role or life what needed to be resolved, what was the problem and what steps you took to resolve the matter?*

What responses are we looking for as HR and as a Company?

- The candidate has done their research
- They have relevant experience, skills, experience or certifications
- They have dealt with customers and understand the basics of customer service
- They are calm and can fix a problem and ask for help when needed

If your child has not got any work experience use examples from school, colleagues, work experience or hobbies.

Best practice is to be prepared for these answers, so I would recommend that your child:

- Jot down some basics from the research that they have done.

- Learn to say "As you can see from my CV at school, college or university, work experience or industry placement I gained relevant qualifications, worked on projects [give examples]. I completed work experience at [place] where I was able to interact with customers and completed projects in [role specific]."

- When applicable, say "In my last role, I [give a customer- or problem-based answer]." When doing this, try and match your answer to a related scenario to the role you are applying for."

Here's an example of how to say this:

"Whenever I have a problem, I understand how big the problem is and how to break it down. I once had a customer problem. I empathised with the customer and recapped what the problem was. I then looked at our policies and ways of working to provide support, in line with company guidelines. This way, I was able to solve the customer issue and they were happy with the outcome."

If your child is required to work on projects, they may get asked, "Have you ever missed a deadline?"

To answer this, they can relate back to school or university if they have ever been close to missing a deadline. What did they do? Did they ask for an extension? What did they learn from that scenario? Why were they going to miss the deadline? "I underestimated how long a [section, module, task] would take. I made sure moving forward that I gave myself enough time or asked for support earlier, so it would not happen again"

Be prepared, even if you don't get asked all the questions, you will have gained real insight into that business and potential role.

Practice, Practice, Practice
The consequences of not being prepared can range from missed opportunities to a dent in confidence. Therefore, it is important that your child practises answering these questions.

I carry out mock interview training with college students right up to executives, and the main issue I hear is waffle, total and utter waffle. Remember what you are being asked, and answer it in the best and most concise way possible. Some people start talking and go totally off on a tangent, that they even have to ask what the question was again. Don't let that be your child.

Nerves play a huge role in interviews. Tell your child that it's a normal response to be anxious: They are going into a new environment, and they aren't 100% sure what they are going to get asked. Some nerves are healthy, and role-playing the interview may feel silly, but a worthwhile cause. A technique I have used for many years is sitting back-to-back with the person you are role-playing with, as it is far less awkward.

If you have prepared some questions, go ahead and bring your notes into the interview. Remember, it's not an exam, so you are allowed to bring out your notes. Again, it shows you have prepared. It's okay to say you are nervous to the interviewer; just take a moment, and I always suggest, if you get offered a drink, say yes. This gives you time to just take that moment, as they won't start the interview until you have a drink. This period often leads to an informal conversation with the interviewer, which will help ease any nerves.

If it is an online interview, pin the notes on the wall next to you so you can use your notes as a prompt.

I have seen some research into techniques and ways to help neurodivergent people be more confident in an interview. And it was as simple as asking the interviewer to provide the questions prior to the interview, or to display (i.e. type them out in the chat) what question was being asked so you could reference it.

Interviewers want nothing more than to find the right person for the job, so if your child approaches the interview with confidence, preparation, and a willingness to communicate their experience and abilities, it will show potential employers that your child is the solution they've been searching for.

Going the Extra Mile

How does your child go the extra mile and maximise their opportunity in an interview to get hired?

First impressions continued: A confident handshake.

Teach your child the proper way to shake the hand of their interviewer: When shaking their interviewer's hand, they should remember not to crush the hand nor to give a limp handshake. They should offer their hand, shoulders back, eye contact made. They should smile and lightly squeeze their interviewer's hand.

Is this a deal breaker?

No. But a weak handshake doesn't say "I am confident," while a hand-crushing handshake feels like they are proving their dominance, which is not a great first impression either.

What if your child gets asked, "Do you have any questions?" They would do well to take that chance. An interview is as much an opportunity for the candidate to understand if the business and the line manager are right for them.

I speak to people who have said I had a gut feeling that the job didn't feel right during the interview, and subsequently this often proved to be correct and they left the position within 6 months.

As a minimum here are a few questions I would recommend should be asked by the candidate:
1. If I am successful, what does my induction look like?
2. After meeting me today, do you think I would be a good fit for the role/company?
3. What are the next steps? Are you interviewing anyone else?

I suggest that your child ask these, as the induction question will offer insight into the structure and timing of their induction. If they start to tell your child about it, "It's a 12-week induction and onboarding, we will teach you about policies, ways of working, etc." Then that is a really positive response.

Asking them question #2 will give your child an idea of how they did and what the potential employers are thinking. They may say that the candidate meets a lot of what they are looking for, but they lack certain skills or experience. This is an opportunity for your child to address those points, if they do have the necessary experience.

Question #3 is about understanding time frames, further processes, technical exams, presentations, as well as other competition your child may have. It's also good to understand when you may hear back from them.

Negotiating Salary

Your child will often get asked "What's your salary expectation?"

I would usually say, depending on how qualified they are in the role determines how much they pitch for. This is why it's important that you encourage your child to review the role they are applying for, what skills they have and how much value they can add to the role and the company. If you have everything they are asking for, ask for the highest possible rate. If you have 80% of the required skills, then go for about 80% of the given salary for the role.

If your child already has a job, they can open with "I am currently on £X and looking for £X." Take the % calculation or go for £3-5k more.

If your child lacks some skills but are willing to learn or get certified, they can say "I am looking at £X because I haven't got those certifications. So I am happy to start on £X, but after my certification, I would be looking at £X."

Some businesses offer conditions a bit like university when you get accepted. "You will start on £X but after probation you will get £X." Or, "if you get a specific certification, you will move to £X."

I will talk more about certifications in Chapter 8, but advise your child to take a copy of their CV as a minimum. If they have certificates, references, recommendations, Duke of Edinburgh certificates, or portfolio, they can hand over this file when the "Please tell me more about yourself" question is asked.

This shows what your child has achieved or allows them to showcase their portfolio.

This can really add value when they are describing themselves, which you haven't been able to showcase in your application. It not only shows you are prepared but have gone a little extra mile.

Finish with thanking the interviewers for their time. Don't forget they have invested or are about to invest thousands in you. It's nice to hear some gratitude.

I would use a simple "Thank you for your time today, I enjoyed the interview and appreciate your time."

Preparation Refinement

When your child has secured an interview, advise them it is important to look at where they are being interviewed. Is it at the office or online at home?

If it is at the office, how long is it going to take them to get there? Can they park nearby? Allow your child to do their research.

If it's at home, they should ensure their background is clear.

True story: I once interviewed someone online, and their underwear was hanging up behind them. It was so distracting. I don't want to see your pants. Clear your background, put up a nice picture, conduct the interview in a quiet area.

Your child also needs to make sure everyone knows they are in an interview and can't be disturbed. Ensure there are no distractions in the background during the interview, otherwise the first impression is that it's not a great homeworking – hybrid working environment, and that you are not going to be productive.

Tell your child to be logged on or in the reception or office 10 mins before the interview. Not 5 or 20! If they arrive too early, they put pressure on the interviewer as you are sitting in reception, and they become distracted.

Ten minutes allows your child to check sound and camera, and message the HR manager if they have connection issues and can arrange a different method.

If it's in the office, encourage your child to be polite to the receptionist; they may be in the interview as well. I often asked my admin or reception team how the candidates were whilst waiting for their interview?

Did they talk? Were they nervous? I wanted to get their first impressions of the candidate.

Advise your child to have a look at the company website. If there are profile pictures, what are they wearing? Are they wearing suits? Are their outfits smart and casual? Your child should try and match the interview they are going for. If they can wear a suit, wear a bright top, tie or pashmina or scarf.

Why? After having interviewed a few people, it's hard for an interviewer to remember exact names. So sometimes if an interviewee has worn something that stands out, it's easier to discuss and they become more memorable. For example, "The chap in the red tie talked really well about...." or "The lady with the yellow cardigan had the right qualifications...."

Whilst I cannot guarantee it will get your child the job, just wearing the right thing and dressing appropriately is a great first impression.

I usually do this when networking. I try to stick to my corporate colours, but often wear a really bright jacket or pashmina. Because if they can't remember my name, they usually say "the blonde lady with the bright scarf."

Helping to guide and practise these skills in interview preparation is an invaluable gift that will serve your child throughout their career. By understanding the reasons, the ways, and the benefits of being prepared, you empower your child to enter the professional world with confidence and competence. Encourage them to embrace interviews not as intimidating hurdles, but as opportunities to showcase their unique potential.

If your child has had a bad interview, try and talk it through, what didn't they like? Try and understand what it was.

Exercise 7

I am going to finish the chapter with a checklist on how to help your child prepare and gain a competitive edge in their interview. Allow them to check this off in preparation for any interview or have a practice on a job advert.

- Look presentable. Match the role you are going for, but dress smartly, wear a bright top, tie or pashmina.
- Research where the interview is, and make sure you turn up early (10 minutes).
- Stand up and shake hands firmly when approached. A firm handshake is a sign of confidence.
- If offered a drink, accept one even if it's water. It gives time to settle in your situation.
- What do you know about the company? Research when it was established, who their customers are, what their mission, vision, values, and goals are.
- "Tell me a bit about yourself": Match the questions to your CV. "As you can see from my CV, I am studying/have studied…." Bring some tangibles, even if it's just a copy of your CV and certificates, it shows you are prepared.

- Prepare these three things: 1) role suitability, experience, and interest in the role; 2) customer service examples; and 3) a problem you have solved.
- When they ask, "Do you have any questions?" Say yes. Ask questions like "How long is the induction? After meeting me today, do you think I would be a good fit for the role or company?"
- Express your appreciation to the interviewer for their time and the opportunity, and set a positive tone for the interview.

Go for it! And please share your child's wins. I absolutely love hearing the success when my clients and people land a job! It's like scoring a goal in sport. The buzz is amazing!

"The secret of getting ahead

is getting started."

– Mark Twain

Chapter 8
A Parent's Role in the Job Search Strategy

As we wrap up this book, I want to assure you that understanding the Six-Step Strategy will empower you as parents to actively support your children in the dynamic digital world of job hunting. This comprehensive approach equips you with the tools and guidance to prepare your children for success in the job market.

Now, let's consider the emotional journey you might experience as parents. Picture the potential worry and frustration if your child faces months of unemployment. On the flip side, envision the immense relief, joy, and pride when your child secures a job in just a matter of weeks.

Straying from this strategic path, even with the best intentions, could inadvertently prolong the job search, impacting both your and your child's emotional well-being. Therefore, embracing and implementing the Six-Step Strategy is crucial to helping you actively navigate this journey with your children.

The Six-Step Strategy: A Recap
Step 1: Clarify aspirations

Before the job search begins, it's essential for your child to understand and articulate career goals. As Confucius wisely said, "Choose a job you love, and you will never have to work a day in your life." Helping your child align their aspirations with their chosen path sets a solid foundation. Your child may have to do a few roles and gain experience in different sectors before achieving your end goal. How much do they need to earn now? Remember to make sure the location of the role is taken into consideration when negotiating salary.

Step 2: Commit to a strategic job search

Companies call job roles a variety of titles, and with little to no actual work experience, it is important that your child searches keywords rather than job titles. Just type in a location and how far you can travel, key words from the industry or area you want to go into, and make sure the role has been posted within seven days. Prime talent is often hired within 10 days.

Step 3: Craft the perfect CV

Crafting an impactful CV is an art. Statistics show that recruiters spend an average of seven seconds reviewing a CV. A well-structured and compelling CV is crucial to grab their attention in this brief window. 85% of larger companies use ATS to screen CVs, emphasising the importance of tailoring CVs with strategic keywords to increase visibility and success to the interview stage.

Step 4: Unlock networking opportunities

Networking is the key to career success. "It's not always what you know, but who you know" that guarantees success. It is very relevant especially now with the amazing ability to connect and work across the globe. Who do you know, who works in what industry or company, or has links to such. A study by LinkedIn revealed that 85% of job positions are filled through networking. Encouraging your child to build and leverage professional connections can significantly enhance their job prospects. LinkedIn is a great tool for connecting and following companies they want to work for in the future. Start early and build a solid network before they leave education. Visiting job fairs is also a form of networking, as they are connecting with potential employers. It's imperative that they come prepared and have their CV on hand whenever they can.

Step 5: Effectively manage applications

The application process can be overwhelming, but statistics from Glassdoor indicate that, on average, each corporate job opening attracts 250 CVs. Supporting your child to manage applications efficiently ensures they stand out in this competitive pool.

They should be prepared to do their homework!

They need to research the company they are applying to understand the business and tailor their application to that role. They need to make sure they are listening to what the employer is looking for, the same as you would if you were buying a new house, car or phone.

If there are certain criteria that are a must and your child doesn't have it, tell them not to apply. If it's desirable, and your child can demonstrate experience, tell them to go for it!

Step 6: Display their competitive edge in interviews

Candidates often fail in interviews due to insufficient preparation, lack of self-confidence, poor communication skills, a limited understanding of the job requirements, an inability to showcase relevant skills, and neglecting to ask thoughtful questions about the role or the company.

In addition to bringing your CV to the interview, it's advisable to carry any relevant certificates, licences, or a portfolio showcasing your work samples or projects, as these supplementary materials can provide a more comprehensive representation of your skills, achievements, and capabilities beyond what is outlined in your CV.

Preparation and practice are key! Practice from first impression handshakes to interview questions. Nerves are normal, accept a drink, take notes and anything else that can help with the interview. Wear something memorable (but not too distracting).

Parental Pitfalls

Despite your well-intentioned efforts, there's a possibility of unknowingly hindering the process for your child. Here's why:

Sharing personal career experiences, while valuable, should not entail imposing personal choices. Each individual's journey is unique, and just because you followed a certain path doesn't mean your child must do the same, whether it's in teaching, medicine, or starting with less-than-ideal jobs.

Understanding that success doesn't always conform to a predetermined schedule is crucial. The journey toward a fulfilling career is a gradual process, not a race. Instead of fixating on immediate job acquisition, consider setting monthly interview goals. By aiming for at least one interview by the second month after leaving school or university, the focus shifts to a strategic approach.

Acknowledging that the road to success involves challenges is essential. Managing frustration when faced with setbacks is a shared responsibility for both parent and child. The journey may require months and numerous interviews. Staying focused and adhering to the strategy is key—it will work!

Best Practices for Supportive Parenting

Embracing the skill of active listening creates a safe space where your child feels truly heard and understood, laying the groundwork for meaningful and effective communication.

As they navigate through a mix of excitement and fear, it's essential to recall our own experiences at that age. But we must also acknowledge how different it is now. You may not have all the answers, but together you will find them. In acknowledging the evolving world, it's crucial to listen to your child without judgement.

Providing guidance without dictating choices empowers your child to make informed decisions and learn from their experiences. As they venture into the professional world with enthusiasm despite a potential lack of experience, coaching and support become invaluable tools. Encourage their choices with love, guiding them towards growth and success.

In the process of aiding your child, leverage your network wisely. Identify individuals who may offer valuable advice or support, not necessarily securing a job directly. Just support in advice or tips. Asking around in your local community or among friends can surprisingly yield beneficial connections. While you might not personally know someone, someone within your network likely does.

Instilling the importance of teamwork in both the job search and future careers develops a sense of belonging and support. Just as you celebrate academic achievements, express your pride in their efforts, motivating them to naturally strive for more. Teamwork and collaboration should be a consistent theme throughout their journey, emphasising the strength of unity and support in every aspect of life.

After Your Child Secures a Job, It's Time to Let Them Be an Employee

Nurturing your child's independence in their professional journey is a pivotal aspect of their personal growth.

Refraining from excessive micromanagement provides them with the opportunity to cultivate the necessary skills to truly own their career path. While you may display a natural concern for your child's well-being, it is vital to empower them to independently manage their career paths, fostering a profound sense of responsibility.

Furthermore, demonstrating understanding and respect for their decisions in shaping their career ensures the acquisition of valuable skills, enabling them to confidently navigate the complexities of their professional journey.

Acknowledge that mistakes are part of the learning process, and offer support and guidance without overshadowing them. Engage in thoughtful discussions, seek advice when necessary, but refrain from representing them in professional matters.

This approach significantly contributes to their maturity level and shapes how they are perceived in the workplace. Remember, your child is employed by the company, and it is the company that pays them.

"Just try new things. Don't be afraid. Step out of your comfort zones and soar."

– Michelle Obama

Conclusion

As we conclude the steps, I extend my heartfelt best wishes to all parents navigating the path of guiding their children through the job search process. Each individual's journey is unique, and your steadfast support makes a world of difference.

As you embark on this next stage with your children, I encourage you to stay connected, share your insights, and reach out if ever you find yourself needing support. The power of shared experiences is immeasurable, and together, we can build a community and network of support.

As a thank you, I invite you to join our unique community of parents introduced to the Six-Step Strategy where I will share FREE CV templates and resources that will help your child get hired. Scan the QR code to access additional valuable resources.

If you ever find yourself stuck or in need of guidance, remember that there are resources available to assist you. Whether it's through the steps shared in these pages or additional support, you have the tools to empower and guide your child on their journey. In the spirit of teamwork, I wish all parents the best! Go for it!

Keep in touch, share your wins and challenges, and know that you're not alone in this journey. I would love to know in the reviews one thing you learned from the book that has helped with your child's career journey.

Here's to the exciting and fulfilling careers awaiting your children, and to you, the supportive parents championing their success. I wish you and your children all the best, and may your paths be filled with growth, understanding, and the pride that comes from witnessing your children grow within their chosen career, or careers!

References

[1] [Page 43]

Georgieva, Kristalina. 14 January 2023. "AI Will Transform the Global Economy. Let's Make Sure It Benefits Humanity", https://www.imf.org/en/Blogs/Articles/2024/01/14/ai-will-transform-the-global-economy-lets-make-sure-it-benefits-humanity

Haan, Katherine. 25 April 2023. "24 Top AI Statistics And Trends In 2024", https://www.forbes.com/advisor/business/ai-statistics/

Howarth, Joseph. 27 March 2024. "57 New AI Statistics", https://explodingtopics.com/blog/ai-statistics

Jones, Padrig. 5 February 2024. "78 Artificial Intelligence Statistics and Trends for 2024", https://www.semrush.com/blog/artificial-intelligence-stats/

S. Matleena. 8 January 2024. "27 AI Statistics and Trends in 2024", https://www.hostinger.co.uk/tutorials/ai-statistics

[2] [Page 61]

Pritchard, Emma-Louise. 20 September 2015. "10 Phrases Employers Hate to See on CVs", https://www.goodhousekeeping.com/uk/consumer-advice/money/a556816/write-a-cv-mistakes/

Notes

Printed in Great Britain
by Amazon

44583746R00099